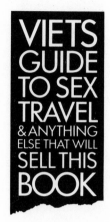

Other books by Elaine Viets

Urban Affairs, 1988.
Images of St. Louis, with Quinta Scott, 1989.

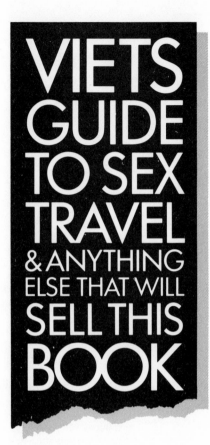

VIETS GUIDE TO SEX TRAVEL & ANYTHING ELSE THAT WILL SELL THIS BOOK

THE PATRICE PRESS
ST. LOUIS, MISSOURI

**Library of Congress
Cataloging-In-Publication Data**

Viets, Elaine, 1950-
    Viets guide to sex travel & anything else that will sell this book.
        p.   cm.
    ISBN 0-935284-72-9 : $17.95
    I. Title. II Title : Guide to sex travel & anything else that will sell this book. III. Title : Guide to sex travel and anything else that will sell this book.
PN4874.V54A25   1989
814'.54—dc20   89-22813
                                                                          CIP

The Patrice Press
1701 S. Eighth Street
St. Louis MO 63104

Printed in the United States of America

With love,
To my South Side grandparents,
Edward and Frances Vierling

Acknowledgments

I wish to thank . . .

Don Crinklaw, my husband, who knows I'd rather have a dozen long-stemmed jokes.

Alana Perez, still the world's best agent.

David Lipman, managing editor of the St. Louis *Post-Dispatch*.

And the cover models:

R. J. Shay, the old traveler.

Jenny Smith, the nice Catholic girl.

Krista Reay, the sexy woman.

Al Huebner, the man by the tire.

Sole man Michael Kilfoy, the feet on the bench.

Jacque Hicks, the Delcia Agency, was the cover cosmetic stylist.

Donald D. Young was the hair stylist.

Photographer Tony Schanuel helped with the lighting.

Paul Dickson, author of "Family Words," gave me valuable advice about writing a second book.

Executive director Glen E. Holt, Anne Watts, and the staff of the St. Louis Public Library were extremely helpful.

Dick Richmond helped with the copy-editing.

The Olympia Broadcasting Networks helped me with the travel section.

My reliable sources, Rich Hinds and Janet Smith, were always on call.

My city hall, police, and other sources who must remain anonymous, are gratefully remembered.

And, finally, thanks to my readers, who gave me these columns.

Contents

Preface

Strange things still happen. Perfectly sensible couples bury plastic statues of St. Joseph upside-down in their front yards to sell their homes—and swear it works.

A Missouri druggist accidentally got a million dollars in gold in the mail.

Another Missourian really does own a car signed by the Beach Boys.

I am a collector and a connoisseur of offbeat stories. Just as small towns in August breed flying saucer sightings, and trailer courts breed tornadoes, my city neighborhood, the South Side, seems to be a breeding ground for wacky stories.

Every city has its version of the South Side—row upon row of neat brick houses, each with a green square of front lawn set in front like a doormat. The people there still live by the old ways: They pay their bills in cash, use their leftovers, and believe fanatically in the virtues of clean, plain living, and just plain cleaning.

But this book also goes beyond the South Side into other subjects: A little sex, a little travel, even a little about when I was growing up Catholic.

If you're a regular reader of my newspaper column, you'll find some of your old favorites, plus something extra—24 columns you've never seen before.

You'll also see another side of me.

Some of the columns I write for the paper have been cut or even killed. Newspapers must, for propriety's sake, censor stories.

Books don't have those limitations.

What you'll read here is the uncensored Viets. No need to get scared. It's only a little bit blue. But I figured you were old enough to hear the risque joke the paper wouldn't print, or know what the racy T-shirt said. And I know you can tackle subjects that still can't be discussed in a newspaper.

I think you're ready to handle it. This is the way grownups talk when the kids aren't around.

So send the children out of the room, settle in and read this book. And if there are any words you don't understand, ask the kids.

Elaine Viets
July 1989

1. Picking Up a Little Something for Mom

We were sitting in the bar of a Chicago hotel, and a pickup was in progress. She was after him. But this was no ordinary chase. What took place in that Chicago bar could affect baby boomers everywhere.

To show you just how classy this place was, the back bar had a bottle of cognac that cost $50 a shot. Even more impressive, the bottle was half-empty.

"I've never tried it," said the bartender. He opened the decanter, sniffed, and said, "Smells sweet, like Courvoisier."

Two young women walked in while the bartender was in mid-snort. They were somewhere in their twenties. One was dark and quiet. The other was curly-haired, bouncy, and funny. The curly-haired one ordered a beer, and every man in the bar fell in love with her.

Curly started talking to the guy on her right. He was a handsome, beefy fifty, proud of his silver hair and expensive suit.

She said she liked to go to all-you-can-eat Sunday brunches. She found one for $15 that had "prime rib, barrels of shrimp and champagne."

"You can eat like that," said Silver, enviously. "You're young."

Then Curly said, "Can I ask a personal question? Are you married?"

"Am I married?" he said, like an echo. "No, I'm not." But he was flattered that such an attractive young woman would ask. He sat straighter and sucked in his gut. The silver fox was turning into a wolf.

Everyone at the bar leaned in to listen. She was back on the subject of brunches. "The first glass of champagne at the brunch was free," she said. "After that you had to pay, except the bartender let me and my friend drink as much as we wanted, and never charged us. I just love buffets. I'm going to try every one in Chicago. Even the ones in the suburbs.

"Do you ever drive to the suburbs?" she asked Silver.

"Yeah, I'll go," he said.

"My mother lives in the suburbs," Curly said. "You'd like my mother. She's better-looking than me. She's thinner, too. She doesn't go to brunches."

"Let me get this straight," Silver said, slowly. "You're interested in this for your mother."

"Yeah," Curly said, cheerfully. "My fiance and I are trying to get her to go out more. Mom's kind of shy. It's hard for her to meet people. We thought of taking out an ad in the personals and screening the calls for her. But you'd be perfect. Are you a lawyer?"

Now the guy was really distressed. "You think I look like a lawyer?" he said. "And you want me for your mother?"

OK, the first encounter didn't go well. But it was a noble experiment. And it shows real promise for aging baby boomers. As we head into our forties, many of us will be single again, for various reasons. And some of our kids will be entering college.

There's not much you can do with kids that age. They eat like horses, they wear fancy clothes, and they're still in expensive schools. In fact, the only thing most college kids are good at is boozing and fooling around.

Why not take advantage of these skills? You sure don't want to go to the bars looking for a date or a mate. The booze does strange things to your waistline and liver.

Why not have the kids pick up a little something for you? I know they'd choose carefully. No kid wants mom married to a geek. They'd look for someone even-tempered, so they wouldn't get hassled. And a guy with some bucks, so he wouldn't cut into their inheritance. And they'd like him to be fun, so they could borrow his Jaguar or use the yacht.

Kids won't be blinded by love, like you were. They won't have you marry some man because you like the way his hair curls on the back of his neck.

And you'll be spared the singles scene. You won't have to listen to stories about his awful ex. You won't have to fight off the bore in the gold chains or console the weepy drunk.

The kids will screen out the losers and deliver the goods, er, ready-made. If you don't have a college-age kid, borrow a surplus child from a friend.

We could even organize these young people into groups, where they would learn about wild life—camping and cruising, and tying knots.

You know—Bar Scouts.

Wait till you try their cookies.

2. *Rhonda and the Sex-Crazed Midgets*

"The problem with being a kid," Rhonda said, "is you never get over it. You never grow up.

"Here I am, thirty-eight years old, divorced, with a kid of my own. But around my father, I still act like I'm a nice sixteen-year-old girl."

That's how Rhonda got in trouble with the sex-crazed midgets.

Rhonda's dad has changed considerably since he was a strict papa.

He's a widower now, living with a woman. "But he treats me like a teenager," Rhonda complains.

"I'm going out with this nice guy named Frank. We're middle-aged, you know, and we like to stay home on the weekends and watch movies.

"Frank doesn't realize how much work even that takes. I had to schlep the groceries, take the kid over to her father's, go to the video store, and pick up three movies. Two were good: *Die Hard* and *The Presidio* with Sean Connery. Then I picked up a porn film. The stores have been picketed in our suburb, so they have removed the movie box covers, and you can't tell how raunchy a movie really is, or what it's about. Some are real dogs."

Literally.

"Mostly, we just laugh at them. But without the covers, you have to play porn roulette and just guess by the title. I was in a hurry. So I picked one called *Ultra-Flesh*.

"The first two movies were good. But *Ultra-Flesh* was a real bust, so to speak. It was so bad, we couldn't even laugh. It had sex-crazed midgets. When the midgets slid under the table, it was too much for us.

"Anyway, Sunday rolled around. Dad and his girl friend were picking me up for a family brunch. I was running late, and I asked Frank to return the three movies.

"I got in Dad's car, and started telling him what a great movie *Die Hard* is. He said he wanted to see it, and he hadn't been able to find it at the video store. So to please Daddy, I ran in and got it from Frank.

"Later that same day I got a call from Dad. He said, 'Are you sure you gave me *Die Hard*?'

"I thought, 'I'm dead.'

"I said hopefully, 'Did the movie have Sean Connery in it?' "

Nope, it had midgets.

"You got it. I'd handed Dad the wrong movie."

Did Rhonda giggle and say she picked a bummer at the video store?

"No, I acted like a teenager caught in the back seat. I squealed, 'Frank picked it out! It wasn't my fault.'

"Since my father has always believed I was the bad one and my sister was perfect, I added, 'And it was Debbie's idea.' "

Rhonda realized from the chilly silence that her father was not amused.

"I called the video store clerk and asked if he'd cover for me. He said, 'Your father was already in. I tried to stick up for you. I told him the guy always gets the porn films.' Even the clerk blamed Frank.

"Frank and my father were just at the first delicate stages of their relationship. Before this, my father was crazy about Frank. He couldn't understand how I'd picked such a nice guy.

"Now Frank is upset because my father thinks he's the kind of guy who rents porn movies about sex-crazed midgets. So he looks all hangdog

and slinks around. This only convinces my father that Frank really does rent those movies. And that I go out with a man who likes sex-crazed midgets.

"You'd still think Dad would be happy. After my first husband, Frank's an improvement.

"It's all my fault. I'm still trying to please my father. And in my eagerness to please one man, I now have two mad at me. If I'd acted like a grownup, this would have never happened.

"Frank is taking it surprisingly well. He didn't yell. He even laughed a little."

He's just been a little short.

3. Move Over, Dr. Ruth

I gave my first sex advice at sixteen. It happened in the girl's bathroom at school. Sandy and I were sitting on adjoining sinks, talking about boys.

Sandy had a date with Mark, the cutest guy in school. She couldn't believe her good fortune.

Neither could I. Sandy had a build like a can of spaghetti and bleached blond hair with black roots. Both her skin and her reputation were slightly spotty.

"Oohhh, Elaine," she said, squeezing her pretty, pink-nailed hands together in anticipation. "He's so cute. I really want to keep him. Should I kiss him on the first date?"

I was shocked.

"Absolutely not," I said.

Sandy followed my advice to the letter. She didn't kiss him on the first date. She got pregnant, instead.

Based on that success, I knew I could help more people. By the time I was in college, I was ready for matchmaking.

My friend Carla looked a little like Sophia Loren. She was black-haired and voluptuous. Her big, brown eyes were like puddles of Hershey syrup.

I knew she'd be perfect for Don H.'s friend, a college professor named David. David was as dry and ascetic-looking as an Old Testament prophet, but he said he wanted a date.

I fixed him up with Carla. I knew it would work out. Carla was cute and cuddly. David was intellectual. They would complete each other. And after they got married (I figured three months was a decent engagement period), their kids would have his brains and her looks. God help the kids if it got reversed, but I couldn't be responsible for everything.

Don H. and I doubled with David and Carla for their first date. It started out OK. David said, "Hello." Carla said, "Hi." They talked about school for awhile.

We went to a Mexican restaurant. David lectured us on authentic Mexican food. Carla looked at the menu and said, "I'll have one of them strawberry DAY-queer-ies."

David turned colder than her daiquiri. The evening went downhill from there.

The next morning, David was on the phone yelling at Don H., "How could you fix me up with someone who was fat?"

"She was voluptuous," said Don H.

"She was FAT," screamed David. "Fat, fat, fat!"

Meanwhile, Carla was calling me. I got the impression the wedding was off.

"I thought we were friends," she wailed. "How could you fix me up with a guy who has a wart on his head?"

What wart?

"The one right on his bald spot. You got me a date with a bald guy with a wart on his head."

Carla finally forgave me. In fact, she even let me blow $150 for a bridesmaid's dress when she married a nice, rich doctor and disappeared into the suburbs.

4. Adventures in Mid-Life Dating, Part I: Veterans Dating Veterans

If second marriages are the triumph of hope over experience, then mid-life dating is even braver. You have no hope and lots of bad experience, but you go ahead anyway.

"It's veterans dating veterans," wrote the battle-scarred Rich Hinds. He's survived one marriage and one live-in lover. He's paid child support and palimony. And now he's back in the dating scene, no longer a hopeful, horny sixteen.

Rich chronicled his adventures in mid-life dating. "It just flowed out of my word processor," he said. "It was a catharsis."

That's a Greek word meaning, "It feels so good when it's over."

"By veterans, I mean both parties have been married at least once, or have had a significant (ugh) relationship."

Freud said there were six people in every lovers' bed. But a mid-life date is even more crowded. "We each come to the date with all our disappointments and emotional scars," Rich wrote. "The innocence of teen dating is gone. So is the patience and tenacity.

"A date is not as exciting any more. This isn't due to fading hormones. They're still there, somewhat diluted. But you're tired of playing the same old games. It doesn't seem quite worth the effort.

"When I was a younger man, I had the SFD, the Standard First Date.

This formula evening got over the opening gambits as quickly and cheaply as possible. The SFD had four elements:

"It started with one perfect rose. Next, a movie, preferably a sex comedy. (Listen if and when she laughs.)

"Then a serious talk over ice cream and tea at a dessert house that played classical music.

"And finally, if luck was with me, a ride that ended in a secluded parking spot. There, we necked.

"Remember necking? You proceeded to neck yourself into a spermatic colic. There was no cure." In those days, when a young man walked his girl to the front door, he was hunched over—and it wasn't because his back hurt.

"In mid-life, there is no Standard First Date. There is no standard. There isn't even an easy way to set up a date.

"None of this, 'I'll pick you up Saturday night about 7.' Now you both have careers, obligations, maybe children. You have to check your calendars: Who has custody of the kids that weekend? Can she get a babysitter? Who has a business trip? An office party? Finally, it's 'Oh, yes, I think I can make it.' "

Now there's a new hurdle: What will we do? And how much will it cost?

"You'd like to say, 'How about a nice, cheap dinner, a few drinks, some sexy conversation, and the sack?'

"That's too easy. A date has to be an event. And it will be, because everything costs so much. Just how much it costs comes as a shock for the mid-life man. A movie, two drinks and a pizza are $30. Dinner at a good restaurant is twice that. You need a bank loan for your love life.

"Instead, you resort to your friends. Some comrade is holding an odd event."

Odds are, it will be cheap. You take her to Fifties parties and openings of ethnic restaurants that have Formica tables and travel posters on the walls.

But first you have to pick up your date. "She always lives in East Nowhere," said Rich.

You break out the map. "Map reading requires two things: your full attention and enough light. You cannot read a map and drive. I haven't found a map yet that glows in the dark.

"You stop in a strange part of an alien suburb, turn on the dome light, unfold the map and pray that it's current enough to have her street. Meanwhile, someone calls the police about the suspicious person in the old car casing the neighborhood."

Maybe your date gave you directions, but you didn't memorize them. "Just try to read your cryptic notes by the dome light. They seemed clear at the time."

Does "turn lt, thrd light, liquor store" mean you should turn left at the third light by the liquor store? Or turn left at the third light AND stop by the liquor store for a bottle of wine?

At least you won't have the humiliation of calling your intended. You can't. You left her phone number at home.

5. *Adventures in Mid-Life Dating, Part II:*
Dancing in the Dark—Your Friends and Your Date

At mid-life, the single man is not a pistol. He is a loose cannon, crashing about. He needs to be tied down. The man needs a mate.

He agrees. He's tired of committing lust in his heart.

In the old days, parents arranged a marriage for you. Today, friends make matches for the mid-life man. These are called blind dates.

Woe to the man who tries to find a woman without a little help from his friends. Just ask mid-life man Rich Hinds.

"Your friends, or those left to you after the custody fight, will put your date under a microscope. They are good at finding the character flaws you overlooked in your fevered state."

So who's more important, your date or your friends?

That's easy, Rich said. "Your friends. They will be with you for years, while your date may only last another evening."

It's better to give in gracefully and let your friends arrange a blind date.

"Blind dates are those things which you promised you'd never go on again," Rich said. "The women you meet on one are always described the same way: Just Wonderful. Bright. Pretty. And Loads Of Fun To Be With."

Calling a woman Just Wonderful, Bright, etc., "never answers the important questions: Will she throw up when she sees a middle-aged fat guy? Does she have anything catching? Can I afford her?

"An over-forty male with a bod like a 50¢ Dairy Queen does not expect a centerfold. But I would like some personality. I'll take compatibility over curves."

Thanks to your friends' descriptions, you don't know what your blind date is like. And she, poor woman, doesn't have a clue about you.

" 'I told her all about you,' your friends say. They really told her about someone else. Friends, like fond parents, are blind to your little faults. Like your habit of sandpapering your toes at the dinner table."

And, like doting parents, they exaggerate your slightest talent.

"My friends told one woman, 'Rich is a terrific dancer.' She saw herself gliding across the dance floor in my masterful arms. The reality was quite a comedown."

Rich wouldn't dream of asking a woman to go dancing. "At least, not when I'm sober.

"Why do men dance? It's been awhile since I wanted to celebrate a fresh bison kill. I don't count that little jig I do when I stub my toe.

"The answer is: Men dance to be close to women. Real close. Unfortunately, most modern dancers don't even touch.

"Slow dancing is different. You get to hold a woman, smell her perfume, and if you're lucky, lead. Dancing with some women is like trying to move a refrigerator across a kitchen—you can't wait till it's over and you hope you won't get hurt."

Slow dancing works best with someone you love. Then you wrap your arms around each other, and move dreamily around the floor. But it's too soon to go this slow with most blind dates. They expect some finesse on the floor.

"She's been told you're Fred Astaire, or at least Tommy Tune. But your skills are slim, even with illegal amounts of alcohol in your system.

"The only dance you're really good at is the Hokey Pokey. She's just finished an Advanced Imperial course at the local high school adult education program.

"Even if you could dance, you wouldn't know where to go. You haven't asked a woman to dance since college, somewhere back in the late Neolithic era. And even that was due to a serious hormonal imbalance. You don't know where the dance joints are."

What do you do when you want to put your best foot forward on a mid-life date?

"Fake an injury," Rich said. "There is much to be said for the lower back, but I prefer the knee or the ankle."

Then you can tell her the truth—you've had problems in the joints for a long time.

6. Adventures in Mid-life Dating, Part III: I Still Have Everything, It's Just Lower

Gypsy Rose Lee said, "I still have everything now I had twenty years ago. Except now it's all lower."

The single mid-life man still has everything he had at twenty. And he's probably wearing some of it. It only takes a few failed dates to realize your old wardrobe is a mistake.

Rich Hinds covers the subject in his mid-life dating guide.

"It's no secret women are more sensitive to dress than most males. Most mid-life men have already concluded we've bought all the clothes we'll ever need. This makes for major trauma when you begin dating. Suddenly, your Hawaiian shirts are suspect and your comfortable shorts are just baggy.

"Ties that seemed all right are too fat or too skinny. Lapels are too wide or narrow. And the polyester-knit suit, once the wonder of science, has a dust line from hanging undisturbed for years.

"Don't forget those wardrobe blunders like the Nehru jacket, that were in for about an hour and a half."

You and your clothes are out of date. What are you going to do about it?

"For most men, clothes shopping is like going to the dentist," Rich said. "You put it off until it gets so bad you can't stand it. You don't really know what to buy because your mother, wife, or girlfriend always told you.

"Now, you're on your own. You don't know the difference between fashion and fad. And you've learned to live with your old wardrobe. You've worked out all the mysteries of coordination. You know what tie goes with the tweed jacket. Your outfits become a series of uniforms. You really resent it when one of the pieces rebels and loses a button or develops a frayed cuff. How can these ungrateful rags do this to you?

"Psychologists say men tend to be less critical of their bodies than women. What they forgot to say was you still think you can dress like you were twenty.

"Wrong. Your body has matured. That means the thin parts are now fat and fat parts are several inches lower. They don't make anything trendy in a size 46. And the prices belong on small appliances, not shirts and ties. It's almost a pleasure to buy underwear. It's so simple. Why isn't underwear a problem? Because you're probably still wearing the same style your mother dressed you in when you were four: White Jockey shorts. And white undershirts. Guys who don't wear undershirts don't have any good rags to wash their cars. They also sweat through their shirts.

"It takes perseverance and a Visa card, but you finally put together one or two outfits that don't look like they should be sent to Goodwill. These will get you through the first few dates. Then you can ease back into your old clothes."

The clothes are new, but it's the same old mid-life man preparing for the date.

"First, you panic. That never changes. Then you clean your teeth and press your shoe laces. You shower for an hour and a half. You select the cologne which will make her your love slave.

"Then you dress with the ceremony known only to mid-life daters and matadors. You both make the same prayers for a clean kill."

And you know, as you go out into the arena, that you could be painfully gored. And not get the tail.

7. *Adventures in Mid-Life Dating, Part IV: The R Word*

Today, we are ready to discuss the R word: Relationship. Rich Hinds says most men classify that word with "chancre, jungle rot, and terminal cancer."

"As soon as you find someone you're fairly comfortable with, you are faced with the R word.

"Relationships pass through three phases: Lust and Hope, Complacency, and The Long Night. In the final stage, the patient is dead, but no one has the courage to turn off the life support.

"The typical relationship lasts two years before The Long Night. This allows you to share several major holidays, birthdays, and Valentine's Days. The first Valentine's Day is traditionally mushy. The second is less so, until The Long Night when the cards and gifts become increasingly comic, the opposite of reality."

You sound so grim, Rich. Relationships, indeed. What about love?

"Love is a fragile commodity, although at one time you thought you had it in infinite supply. I think that was January of 1962. One day, it's not there. You no longer think of love at all. Now it's comfort."

But mid-life dating is anything but comfortable. "There was the terrific tall gal with the two kids. You ignored the smelly little vermin because she had those exciting long legs and a reputation for 'just wanting to have some fun.' She passed out in your friend's bathroom with the door locked. You never saw her again.

"What about the beautiful woman you wined and dined? She said she was so broke she hardly had gas money. You said, 'Don't worry, I'll fix you dinner.' At least, she wouldn't pass from this world without a good meal. Then you found out she owned half the city.

"Who can forget the newly divorced blonde? Her problems with her kids sounded like a great plot for a miniseries. Actually, it was two blondes, but the tragic stories melted into one nightmare.

"Or the woman who promised that as soon as you were truly free of the last relationship, you could go out with her and it would be 'simply gangbusters.'

"Well, you got free and said, 'Let's go!' And she told you she's not that kind of woman. She said, 'Couldn't we just be friends?' That phrase ranks with, 'My mother doesn't want me to go out with you' as one of the great put-downs. You don't even know her mother.

"You have very few female buddies. But you have lots of women you're too scared to try for because you're a coward or their boyfriends drive Broncos with rifle racks.

"There are also the women you've tried for and missed but keep hoping to get. Their 'just friends' line kills any hope and puts you just below lepers as a romantic interest."

You now have many situations, all of them hopeless, but not serious.

"Juggling is a problem. As a callow youth I once had four—count them, folks, four—girlfriends at one time. I thoughtfully placed them in different parts of the city, each at a different school. I cheerfully made dates and kept them straight, even managing the holidays.

"No more. Now I can't manage more than one at a time. I keep seeing these nice women who look like fun. Maybe, just maybe, they're Ms. Perfect, but oh, hell, what's the use?

"I have a vision of the woman I could love and live with," Rich said, "but either she doesn't exist, or the wait will be long. Therefore, I'm abstaining from the hunt. I have become Brother Tim, a veteran of the mid-life dating wars.

"I just went on my first date as a fifth wheel, and it wasn't half-bad. I wasn't part of a couple. But I also knew the rules. There were no surprises or letdowns.

"The new Brother Tim will try to be witty, drink enough brandy to make the ache subside, and wait."

Editor's note: Friends report that Brother Tim disappeared while Rich was on a date with a delightful woman.

They do not have a four-door, chrome-plated relationship yet, but they seem to be having an awfully good time.

8. Divine Love

One Saturday afternoon, Wanda was hanging around the Shaw Park pool in Clayton with some friends. A guy jumped up and said, "I'm going to church."

Another young man stood up and said, "I am, too."

Wanda was surprised by this unexpected show of devotion, but decided to join the crowd. "Maybe I'll go with you," she said.

"Oh, no, you don't," said the young man. "You'll cramp our style."

Lord save us. "They were scouting for girls," Wanda said. "Church is the newest place for singles. I'm Catholic. I go to Mass. But my friends in other religions say it works for them at their churches, too."

Forget the bars, personal ads, and supermarkets. You can meet the most divine people in church. Wanda says some singles in their late twenties believe church is the safest place to find a date.

"You learn a lot about someone who goes to church. You can find out his religion, his finances, where he lives, and how generous he is. And if he's at church you assume he has some values."

Wanda stopped and thought a minute. "Well, maybe, even if he's there to find someone. I mean, it's not like he's going to a bar."

When the collection basket is passed, you get a look inside his wallet—and his heart. "I always notice if a guy doesn't put anything in the collection basket," she said. "It's not classy."

But there's a right way to meet Mr. Right, even in church. "Timing is important," Wanda said. "You have to find out what service the young crowd goes to. I was going to morning Mass, but I didn't see any single guys. Then I found out that's when they're all out jogging. Young men go to church in the evening. I switched to 5 o'clock.

"Picking the right church is important, too. I live in Clayton, and I prefer to go to the ones in my area. At first, I went to a church in Brentwood, but then my friends said Immacolata on Clayton Road was the place to be.

"I've been dressing up, too. I've gone from wearing pants to a skirt. Of course, you don't want to overdo it. Then you look like you're looking."

And never join a church singles group. "Those are hopeless," Wanda said. "But the choir might work. Our choir is full of women, so it's a better opportunity for men."

Wanda says during the sermon is a good time to check out the church. "I listen with one ear while I watch the guys."

I don't know how to say this exactly, but how do you pick up someone in church?

"You start a conversation with them afterward. It's best to show up a little bit late. Then you can stand in the back, spot an interesting man and sit next to him. I kept watching this one man during the service, and he kept watching me. Afterward, I said, 'Hi, how are you?'

"He said, 'Hi.'

"I said, 'Do I know you?'

"He said, 'Do you go to Houlihan's?'

"I said yes, just to keep the conversation going. We wound up going out. It didn't work out, but at least I tried.

"I don't know what God would think, but my mother used to say I could meet a nice boy at church. She was right. You just have to know how to go about it."

The Lord works in mysterious ways. I checked with the pastor of Immacolata church to see if he noticed business was picking up.

Monsignor Russell J. Obmann said, "Our 5 o'clock Sunday Mass is a strange one. There are about fifty people there from our parish—and 750 from around the West County area. They come in late and leave early. They're predominately younger people. But whether they're married, single, or divorced, I can't tell you."

He does know this bunch throws their pennies around like manhole covers.

"This is the largest Mass we have, and it's when we get the least amount of contributions. There are a handful of envelopes from our parishioners, and then quarters, nickels, and dimes. I've never seen anything bigger than a buck in the collection basket, and not many of those.

"If singles are coming here, they have to sit down and participate in the service. Whether I'm running a dating bureau or not—I don't know what to say."

How about "Let us prey"?

9. Everything You Were Afraid to Ask About Your Wedding

Many of you will become engaged and start planning the perfect wedding. Take my advice. The only perfect wedding is when you elope.

But you won't listen. I didn't.

You think if you don't have a big wedding you'll be missing something. You will: Fights, tears, nervous breakdowns, and massive debts.

Wedding guidebooks won't help you. They may tell you who pays for the flowers and how to address the invitations, but they ignore the really important things. So I'll tell you. I've devised a special wedding guide. It's called:

What No One Else Will Tell You About Your Wedding

Where to hold the traditional fight with your mother: For brides who want an intimate affair, there's no place like home. Start three hours before the wedding, so the whole family can join in.

Other brides prefer a large bash. In that case, the best place is the bridal shop. If there are lots of strangers around, this is a good time to announce you are pregnant.

Invitations: No matter how hard you try, at least one of your wedding invitations will go astray in the mail. And it will usually be the one for your evil-tempered aunt. She will be sure you did it on purpose.

Take comfort in this. It could be worse. In the old days, she would have turned you into a frog.

Wedding gifts: Duplicate wedding gifts that can't be returned (toasters, ice buckets, bun warmers) make excellent presents when your friends get married. But some presents are too ugly to pass on. The winner at my wedding was a set of gold fruit spoons, covered with wart-like excrescences that turned out to be plums and pineapples.

Do not despise these ugly gifts. They can be pawned to buy useful household items, such as six-packs and pepperoni pizzas.

Wedding dresses: Make sure you order a dress several sizes too small. This is your last chance to diet down to the size you want to be. A strict diet will make those last weeks before the wedding even more exciting. It also does remarkable things to your temper.

Here's another tip: Always order your dress in white satin. That way it will show all the needle marks for alterations.

And, speaking of changes, you must have figured out why many wedding gowns have such high waists, no matter what the fashion. A "premature" baby is no disgrace any more. Most parents are grateful if the couple marries at all. But it does provide hours of harmless fun for people who like to count backward on their fingers.

Bridal registry: Be sure to ask for the most expensive china, crystal and silver patterns—the ones where whole families club together to buy a butter knife. That way, when your youngest child drops the butter knife down the garbage disposal twelve years later, you can't afford a new one.

Bachelor party: Forty years ago, a bachelor party was a disgusting male ritual on the eve of a sacred ceremony. Often, the groom would get drunk with his friends and leer at a female stripper.

Today, we are more enlightened. Now, the bride can get drunk with her friends and leer at a male stripper.

Marriage, length of: For better or worse, marriages don't always last till death do us part any more. But it's good etiquette to stay married at least until your parents have paid for the reception.

10. Some Stranger Has Seen You Naked

Not long ago the great Peeping Tom scandal at the Cervantes Convention Center was in the headlines. Someone in security secretly videotaped young models dressing for a fashion show.

A local TV station was so outraged by this violation of the women's privacy, they ran the tape. The women's bodies were obscured by a checkerboard effect, but you could still figure out one model wasn't wearing any underwear.

Every man and woman who shops has been spied on in stores. Everyone who drooled over those innocent models on that TV tape has had their own lumps and bumps watched by strangers.

But when you're watched today, it's not voyeurism, it's legit. It's done in the name of security. You've been videotaped in parking garages and bank lobbies. You've been spied on through two-way mirrors in department stores and discount houses. Sometimes, signs on the store walls clearly announce the peeping policy.

"For your protection. . . ." they start out nobly, but the message comes through loud and clear. When you shop here, we'll watch your every move.

So what? You've got nothing to hide. You're just shopping. And scratching, yelling at the kids, rooting around in your purse, and picking your nose.

And somebody making $3.50 an hour is watching and maybe taping you. What happens to those tapes? You'd better hope they were destroyed. But there's no guarantee. How do you know you aren't in some weird employee's home movie?

Strangers have also seen you in your underwear. I know. I was one of the people checking you out. In the late sixties, I worked at a "better dress shop" in a suburban shopping center. The dresses sold for $50 to $200.

If the store manager didn't like the look of a customer, we were sent back to the dressing room to "help" her. Almost anything could trigger the manager's suspicions.

Maybe the customer didn't dress well enough. Maybe she dressed too well and wore too much perfume. Then the manager thought she was a hooker. And all black customers were suspect, no matter how they looked.

Many customers wanted assistance, and asked for it. But we weren't asked. We followed them, yelled, "Need any help?" and walked in uninvited on folks in their Fruit of the Looms.

We offered to zip them up or get another size, but it was really a form of spying. It's perfectly legal, and the last time I was there, the dress shop was still doing it. The customers never protested or complained. They didn't know what kind of "help" they were getting.

We never caught anyone getting away with anything worse than a little padding in her bra. And when shopping center security finally caught two shoplifters, they didn't fit the store manager's criminal profiles.

One was a fat woman who had rolled up an expensive coat and dress, stuck them between her legs and waddled out the door.

The other was a mother who came in with a crying baby. While the kid distracted everyone with his screams, Mom shoved merchandise in the stroller.

Elegant shops are not the only ones with their eyes on you. Peepholes are a hazard in crummy bars, lonesome truck stops, and isolated country gas stations. If you see the warning signs—lots of grimy black dirt, no soap, no toilet paper and walls painted hospital green or battleship gray— start looking for a peephole some pervert has bored through the wall, and plug it up.

Why do you think truck stop waitresses chew gum?

11. Why the Miniskirt Won't Come Back

I know why the miniskirt failed this time around. I knew the answer after I tried on my old mini from the sixties. Seeing if you can still wear your old miniskirt is one of the great baby boom rituals. It's like trying on an old army uniform.

Sure enough, if I sucked in my gut and didn't breathe, I could wear it. But when I looked in the mirror, I got a nasty shock.

Mom was right. That skirt was too short to wear in public. I have belts with more material. I could repeat the old mini tirades by heart. They were longer than the skirt: "You're not going out like that, young lady, and embarrass this family. No decent cocktail waitress would dress like that. Your whole rear end is hanging out."

I automatically reached down and tugged at the skirt. Then I remembered something else. That's how I spent the sixties. I went straight from pulling up my knee socks to pulling down my miniskirt. It was a drag trying to board a bus, reach into a bottom file drawer, or sit at a lunch counter.

But nobody ever wore a miniskirt for comfort. We wore it for the shock value. After you riled up your parents, you could spend a delightful day upsetting teachers and old ladies of both sexes.

Oh, yeah, one more thing: Miniskirts knocked the boys dead.

But when they returned this time, they played to a different audience. Some young girls bought the skirts for fun, but they won't be the emblem of a whole generation. They don't shock much any more.

A surprising number of boomers can still wear miniskirts. But why?

Now it doesn't bother us to admit Mom was right. At least, maybe a little bit, sometimes.

And there are lots more interesting ways to get the guys' attention.

So the miniskirt got short shrift when it tried a comeback. But its failure had nothing to do with too much media attention, bad retailing, poor consumer marketing, or conservative buyers.

In the sixties, we wore miniskirts because our mothers hated them and men liked them. But we never wore them for ourselves.

When we tried that, they were no big deal.

12. Two-Timing Lover

Love may be grand, but when it goes, that torrent of passion can turn into a river of venom. When you're in love, you want to give him everything. When you split, you argue over who keeps the shrimp forks.

Sometimes, the great romance degenerates into petty acts of revenge: sugar in the gas tank, midnight hang-up phone calls. Worst of all, they're not even original.

That's why this story is so unusual. It's about an ex-boyfriend who got revenge with a parking meter. I heard it from David, who works in a downtown office.

"There's a way to jam a city parking meter with a quarter, but I won't tell you," David said, "because all the ex-es in St. Louis will be running around the city with rolls of quarters.

"Once you jam the meter, you can park free all day—unless the meter maid gets wise. The smart ones flip the handle and find out you've been jamming. Then you get a ticket. It's twenty bucks for jamming a meter.

"There's a woman who works in my office downtown. She parks her car at a meter and feeds it all day. She came out to put more money in the meter, and found she had a $20 ticket for jamming the meter. But she didn't do it. She couldn't figure out what went wrong, but she paid anyway.

"The next day, she got another $20 ticket. Again, she didn't deserve it. Now she's out $40. She wanted to find out what's going on.

"The next morning she parked in the same area, put in her quarter and enlisted two people from the office. They all watched her car out the window. Well, along comes this guy. He went up to her car, took out another quarter and jammed the meter. It's her ex-boyfriend. He's crawled out from under a rock somewhere, and he's getting even with her.

"The building elevators are old and slow. Before she could get downstairs, she had a third $20 ticket. Now he's cost her sixty bucks. But this time she's going to plead not guilty. She's got witnesses."

St. Louis parking meters are under city treasurer Larry Williams. Meter jamming "happens all the time," he said. "It's a very common practice."

Most people jam the meters to escape a parking ticket. A few do it for revenge.

"If you have evidence that a boyfriend, a jilted lover or an enemy is doing this to you, we want to know," Williams said. He said the fine is so steep because "jamming burns out the meter's timer. Each jammed meter runs us about $8."

Here's something else you didn't know. Williams said the three big jamming areas are the downtown post office, the Missouri-Pacific Building and the State Office Building—the Wainwright Building.

"The people who work in those buildings try to park free. We have a team of people watching those areas. And we have photographs."

As for the downtown woman who caught the meter jammer, "three cheers for her," Williams said. "I hope she prosecutes. I'll do anything I can to help her."

There you have it—a happy ending to a timeless tale.

13. *What Every Young Man Should Know*

It was the night before Jeff's wedding. Don H. was telling the groom everything a young man ought to know. After all, he'd successfully survived seventeen years of marriage. He took the trembling lad by the shoulder, sat him down, poured him a beer, and began in a confidential tone.

"The most important thing a married man needs to remember is there are thirty-seven anniversaries and forty-seven birthdays each year. And if you forget one, she'll crack your skull."

"I've already found that out," said the groom.

That's so unfair. I never cracked a skull. I just sulked for several days and asked him if he still loved me.

A man has to remember only four days a year at the most: Your birthday. Your wedding anniversary. Valentine's Day. And Christmas. Is that so much?

Don H. said, "But I like to buy you presents when I feel like it, not because I have to."

So why don't you feel like it on our anniversary?

"It's so regimented."

Regimented is the right word. It's total war if you forget, bud.

It took me a while, but I finally figured out the main difference between men and women: Most men can't remember special occasions. Most women never forget them.

I don't know why men have such a rough time remembering. Surely the angry scenes their mothers had with their fathers are indelibly engraved in their minds.

Whole industries were built on men's forgetfulness. Remember the yellow candy boxes called Whitman's Samplers? About twenty-five years ago, they were marketed as a marital aid. The sole reason Whitman's Samplers used to be sold by the cash register at the drug store was to save marriages. In the olden days, most stores didn't stay open late. But a forgetful husband could always grab a box of candy at a drugstore or neighborhood bar.

Finally, the sampler became identified with forgetfulness itself. I still remember one aunt bursting into tears when my uncle handed her a Whitman's Sampler on their anniversary.

"Drugstore candy," she wailed. "You forgot again."

Of course, it's different when I forget a special occasion. Don H. won't mind, right? But other people might. Like the twelve-year-old kid who asked me, "What are you getting Don for Valentine's Day?"

He's in California. He won't be home for Valentine's Day.

"So what are you giving him when he gets home?"

Me, I said. It was time the kid learned grownups don't give serious answers all the time.

"Why don't you give him something he hasn't had before?" said the kid.

14. Tales That Are Hard to Bear

If you think this is a high-tech age and science has banished superstition, then you've never been pregnant.

"You won't believe the old wives' tales I've heard," Nancy Pearce said.

And some of these old wives are educated young women.

"I never expected these things would survive into the twentieth century. When I had morning sickness, people told me, 'The sicker you are, the healthier the baby.' Great. I have to feel guilty unless I'm barfing my brains out.

"I've heard if you crave sweets, the baby is a girl. If you want spicy foods it's a boy. And if you get a big scare, the baby will have a mark on it."

What kind of mark?

"They never say. It's just one ominous sentence, 'The baby will be marked.'

"They told me if the kid kicks a lot it's a boy. But here's the worst one: If you look glowing, you'll have a boy. If you look lousy, the baby's a girl, because a girl saps your beauty for herself."

What if you're ugly to begin with?

"I think it's relative."

But it's not the relatives who come out with these ugly comments. It's people Nancy barely knows.

"Some want me to start teaching the baby in the womb. They say I should listen to great music through headphones. I'm in law school, so I guess the kid is going to learn torts and contracts. Personally, I wish my mother had listened to algebra tapes. I could have used some help.

"Ever since I got pregnant, I'm public property. Strangers come up to me and rub my stomach. I feel like a lucky Buddha in a Chinese restaurant.

"Nobody looks me in the eye any more. They stare at my stomach. Now I know how Dolly Parton feels. Well, sort of.

"Then there are the kind people who make comments on my appearance. They say, 'You look like hell.' Or, 'Wow, you've really got that old pregnant waddle.'

"And everyone has a compelling urge to tell you some delivery horror story. They always preface it with, 'I shouldn't tell you, but . . .'

"But they do. One said her sister was ripped from ear to ear. And it felt like sitting on barbed wire for a week.

"Last weekend I wore these cute shoes, and someone told me, 'You better wear those now. In a few months your feet will swell like tree trunks.'

"My hairdresser said my hair would probably fall out. Someone else said I would lose a tooth for every baby.

"So here I am. I waddle. I'm hairless, toothless, and walking on tree trunks."

Sounds like a good time to be a man.

"No, even my husband gets dumb comments. He was getting his hair cut last Saturday. The shop was really crowded. The stylist asked him at the top of his voice, 'So. Are you going to breast feed?' "

15. Hitting on the New Mother

When Nancy Pearce was pregant, the human race had an almost irresistible urge to rub her stomach.

"I figured once I had the kid, my life would change."

Oh, baby, did it ever. Strangers quit patting Nancy. Now they hit her with advice.

Before you ask the inevitable question, it was a girl, born June 1, 1988. Her name is Rachel, and she weighed 6 pounds, 15 ounces.

"Everyone is an instant expert on your baby," she said. "Rachel gives one whimper and the unsought advice starts."

The experts say:

"She's hungry."

"She's cold."

"She's sleepy."

"She needs her diaper changed."

"Sometimes they say it all at once. And with such authority. They've been with Rachel five minutes, but they know more about her than I do. They never ask me if she's been fed recently. They just pronounce: 'She's hungry.'

"I'm tempted to answer: 'Hungry? What a great idea. David, when did we last feed her? Was it Thursday or Friday?' "

Then there are the temperature mavens. If the baby cries, they automatically say:

"She's hot."

"She's cold."

"Her feet are hot."

"Her feet are cold."

"Her head is chilly."

"Her head is sweaty."

"When David and I were young and lacked confidence (two months ago), we'd jump at every temperature suggestion, whipping the baby's hat on and off. We finally quit.

"If I put her in the sun, the experts say she'll burn. If I take her out of the sun, they say she needs sunshine for vitamins. If I let people hold her, they warn she'll be overstimulated. If I don't, they say I should because it will get her used to strangers. If she's sleeping contentedly, they tell me she's in a bad position and I should turn her over.

"Then there's the 'good old days' routine. It starts out, 'We never had that . . .' They didn't use disposable diapers. They walked twelve miles in the cold to wash out diapers by hand in an icy stream.

"Whatever the advice is, they absolutely know for sure."

And they believe in it passionately. "Pacifiers start heated debates. The pro-thumb people say a pacifier will ruin Rachel's teeth. They warn she'll take it to college. They say she should learn to suck her thumb because she'll never lose it and it won't fall on the floor.

"Then there are the pro-pacifier people. They rage about how thumb-sucking will ruin her teeth."

Nancy doesn't know why she gets all this advice. "It's not like we walk around in rags. Rachel doesn't have any holes in her clothes. I'm in law school. David has his own business. And thanks to the grandparents, we have every conceivable baby toy and convenience. But people can't resist."

Even the simplest questions are traps. "They always ask me, 'Does she sleep through the night?'

"You could look at my eyes to see the answer is no. But I tell them. Then they want to know if she's on cereal. What age to feed her cereal is another big debate. If I say she's not on cereal, they tell me she'd sleep through the night if I gave it to her.

"Age, politics, and income have nothing to do with it. Young or old, male or female, everyone has the right to advise you. The La Leche League sympathizers are horrified I'm not nursing. They ask the most personal questions.

"To placate some relatives, I may cover up Rachel when they claim she's cold. God forbid she should quit squeaking. Then they're puffed with success. I'm tempted to pinch my own child and make her cry.

"I know now this will never stop. When she's sixteen, I'll still be getting advice. And if anything's wrong, it's going to be my fault. I shouldn't have given her that pacifier."

16. *The Weekend Diamond*

"It happens about once a year," said Harry Schukar. "We call it the Weekend Diamond."

Harry, known to his friends as Buzzie, sells diamonds. He's president of the wholesale diamond division of Harry Winston, the New York company that keeps Liz Taylor in diamonds. Harry Winston could do the same for you. There's an office in St. Louis.

The Weekend Diamond has several interesting facets. "It happens when a woman twenty-five or younger comes in with someone who could be her father or grandfather—but isn't," Buzzie said.

Do old men still buy diamonds for young women?

"Yes. I'm not being chauvinistic. But they always have, and they probably always will. There are still women who won't play ball without the diamonds."

There are still young women who hunt silver foxes, the nice name for rich, randy old duffers.

"This is a very small part of our business," Buzzie said. "About 99.9 percent buy engagement rings and anniversary presents. My favorite are the young engaged couples. They're so in love. But you don't want to hear about them, do you?"

No. Tell me about the Weekend Diamond.

"The couple, the older man and the very young woman, come in. It's typically after 2 o'clock on Friday. There's a reason for that. The banks are closed. He says they want to pick out a piece of jewelry. They look and pick and settle on something."

Is it expensive?

"We have nothing under $50,000 in our showroom. It ranges from $50,000 to $250,000, although we do have more expensive jewelry."

Buzzie said that with a straight face.

"He says he wants to pay by check. He knows we won't let anything that expensive out until we've checked with the bank. And he knows the bank is closed until Monday."

But it would be crass for a class jeweler to mention these ugly facts. "So we say, 'We don't want to sell a fine piece of jewelry in this condition, sir. We'd like to check the clasp and clean it for you. We'll have it for you on Monday.'

"She's disappointed. But he doesn't argue. That's the real tipoff." They leave together, in a state of delightful anticipation.

"On Monday he returns without the young woman. He usually comes in about 11 o'clock. He says, 'I'm Mr. Jones, and I selected the diamond jewelry on Saturday.'

"We say, 'We're sorry, sir, but there weren't enough funds in your account to cover the check.' Actually, we don't even bother to call the bank. We know there aren't.

"He says, 'Oh, you know that. But it sure was a great weekend.' "

The silver fox was a rat.

17. Growing Up Catholic

God made me to know, love, and serve Him, and be happy with Him in heaven.

God made me pretty nervous. I could be recalled at any time, like a defective car.

We learned this in catechism class in a Catholic school. But there were certain other things we picked up in the alleys of the Catholic faith.

Like guardian angels. We were told God gave us a guardian angel to watch over us. These heavenly bodyguards were issued automatically at birth, like rifles in the army.

We were also taught that angels did not have bodies and did not take up physical space, but somehow that part didn't sink in.

In the first grade, we lived with a whole angel mythology. God knows where it came from, but we believed guardian angels were big suckers wearing gauzy drapes, with white wings the size of grand pianos. If necessary, they could produce flaming swords and send Satan on his way.

The last thing you wanted was to tick off your guardian angel. And so, at about age six, you had the terrible problem of making room for your guardian angel. It was easy to scooch over in your desk, so he could have a seat in class. At night, if you hung onto the railing in your bunk bed, he could catch a nap.

But the real problem was making room for your angel in church.

You knew that angels always sat on the right side. The devil sat on the left. So, while your teacher was trying to put as many people as possible into the pew, you were trying to make room for your angel on the right, and squeeze out the devil on your left. And if you were sitting next to Timothy Mettermann, you didn't want to leave room anywhere. That kid had the devil on all sides.

It was a complex problem, and the Sunday sermons were no help. The pastor rarely discussed angels. He was too worried about the bill collectors breathing down his neck.

The guardian angel seemed to disappear about the time we studied sin. We learned that there were two kinds of sins: venial sins, which were little and were speckled all over your soul like freckles on Mary Alice Figby's face.

And mortal sin, the biggie. That turned your soul pitch black. Die with an unrepented, unconfessed mortal sin on your soul and you would go straight to hell. If you got hit by a car after committing a mortal sin and before Saturday confession, you were going to burn forever.

"Remember the pain when you burned yourself on the stove?" said the nun.

We did.

"Multiply that by a million times and imagine it all over your body."
We did.

"That's what it will be like to burn in hell forever," she said, touching off nightmares and outbreaks of bedwetting for weeks.

For Catholic kids, there was only one kind of sin powerful enough to lure us into the terrors of hell—sex.

In addition to actually sinning, there were Occasions of Sin, those gilded pathways to hell. Almost anything could be an occasion of sin. Thinking dirty thoughts was an occasion of sin. So was reading dirty magazines, which would cause you to think dirty thoughts. And hanging around stores that sold dirty magazines. Or hanging around the people who hung around the stores that sold dirty magazines.

Certain nuns provided us with helpful ways to avoid occasions of sin.

French kissing was a for sure mortal sin. You should kiss with your teeth clenched, so his soft searching tongue couldn't get in. If it did, you should bite it off. (No, Dr. Freud, I didn't see anything symbolic about that.)

If you were coming back from the football game and had to ride in a crowded car, you should not sit on a boy's lap. That would cause him to get aroused, and that would be your fault. Therefore, you should carry along the Yellow Pages, and put it between you and the boy.

That might cause some pain, but not as much as burning in hell for all eternity.

I never knew anyone who used Ma Bell's book as a chaperone. Just like I never knew anyone who carried a dime to call her parents in case a date abandoned her because she wouldn't put out. We would rather burn for all eternity than face the black wrath of our fathers when we made a midnight phone call beginning, "Hello, Daddy, I'm in a cornfield off Shackelford Road and Johnny left me. . ."

But we all believed that practically anything could get a teenage boy aroused (which was true) and it was our fault (which was not true) and that boys had no self control and would leap all over us once this happened and we were helpless to stop them.

"We were like little walking Hoovers," said my friend Betty. "We just walked by and an irresistible force made it pop right out of the guy's pants. I was afraid to get near one."

If that wasn't bad enough, we also had to contend with the Domino Theory of Dating. This divided the female body into zones, and one-by-one they fell until BINGO! the boy got the ultimate prize—your virginity—and you were damned forever. Here on earth no nice man would ever marry damaged goods.

Your downfall started innocently enough—a couple of goodnight kisses on the front porch. Then some kissing in the car. Then horizontal kiss-

ing. Then he touched your bosom (clothed). Then he got your blouse off.

By the time he had removed your bra and started working his way down toward your waist, you were on the road to perdition.

We believed in the Domino Theory of Dating, just as we believed in the Apostles Creed.

And so it was a great shock when the head cheerleader, who was going steady with the captain of the basketball team, announced in religion class that she and her boyfriend liked to neck in the back seat because they couldn't afford to go to the movies.

We couldn't conceive, if you'll pardon the pun, of anyone talking about sex in such a lighthearted manner. There she was, risking her immortal soul, not to mention her reputation, because he couldn't scrape up two bucks for a movie.

And secretly we wondered, where was the guilty thrill when sex came in second to *The Sound of Music?* They could almost be married or something.

One great deterrent to sex was our high school uniforms. They were exceptionally ugly. Their gray color turned your skin a mottled reddish white. The A-line skirts with the pleated front panels and the short boxy jackets gave you the graceful lines of a refrigerator. It was difficult to fancy the tenderest young neck, when it was sticking out of a sexless Peter Pan collar. I didn't like his peanut butter, either.

Kathy, the girl at the next locker, was one of the few people who actually had a bosom in that getup. She would have stuck out in front if she wore a cardboard box.

She was a chubby, sweet-faced girl with enormous breasts. I envied her that 40D cup, but she regarded it as a curse and would have gladly given me half so she wouldn't have to wear hefty four-hook bras, like an old lady.

We both made one desperate effort to look like young women. We tried to contrive a miniskirt out of this sexless outfit.

This was the late sixties, when miniskirts were in full (or rather, skimpy) bloom. We had a strict dress code. Uniform skirts must touch the ground when we knelt. We made ourselves instant minis by rolling up the skirt at the waistband.

The nuns knew what we were up to, and would patrol the halls, yelling "Kneel."

If you were really quick, you could unroll your skirt before you hit the ground.

Kathy and I always checked each other's skirts, to make sure they were ready to roll.

It was from her I learned the real consequences of the Domino Theory. There were worse things than losing your soul.

Just after Christmas, Kathy didn't bother to roll up her skirt any more. She also started getting fatter. But just around the middle.

She let out one pleat.

Then she let out a second pleat.

Then she left school to visit her aunt in Michigan. In January.

I never saw Kathy again.

18. What Johnny Carson Did to Mrs. Mettermann

I liked Johnny Carson. But I never thought he was better than sex.

Not that I knew anything about sex in 1964. I was fourteen years old and Johnny Carson was the hottest thing on television.

At work and at school, everyone talked about what they heard on Johnny Carson last night. If you didn't know Johnny's monologue, you lived in social Mongolia.

I couldn't admit I had to go to bed after the 10 o'clock news. So I went upstairs to my room, turned off the lights, and sat by the furnace duct next to my dresser. I could hear the family room TV there.

That's how I listened to Johnny Carson's monologue every night. My parents' laughter sometimes drowned out the next joke, but I picked up enough to get by.

That's also how I eavesdropped on my mother's friends. When they gathered in her kitchen for coffee, the talk got interesting if the kids weren't around.

I learned that Shelley's premature baby weighed 9 pounds, 6 ounces.

That young Mrs. Meyer met the mailman at the front door in her bathing suit. In the middle of winter.

And Mrs. O'Hara, the transplanted Southern belle, left her vacuum cleaner out in the middle of the living room for her husband to carry to the upstairs closet, for God's sake, like she was some kinda cripple.

Funny, the women said, she could haul in those dress boxes without any help.

Then, one day, Mrs. Mettermann confessed that she had figured out a way to watch Johnny Carson while she and her husband . . . you know . . . did it . . . during Johnny's monologue. She didn't miss a joke, and Jim never guessed a thing.

Between the shrieks and giggles, I couldn't figure out exactly how she managed it. But it had something to do with putting the TV on the chest of drawers, and moving her left foot forward.

If Johnny could have seen through the TV screen, his wicked, skinny eyebrows would have arched even higher.

When the giggles died down, another woman, Mrs. Figby, said she also found Johnny Carson useful. She talked her husband into staying up for the monologue every night. Johnny left him weak with laughter. He could barely make it up the stairs, and when he hit the bed he went straight to sleep, no fooling around.

After all, he had to get up at 6 A.M.

This set off another round of giggles and snickers.

And it left me puzzled.

I was sure both these women liked sex. After all, Mrs. Mettermann had five kids. And Mrs. Figby had four.

Mrs. Mettermann was kind of scrawny, but her husband was well-preserved for a man going on thirty-five.

Did this mean Johnny Carson was better than sex?

But sex was such a powerful temptation, the Church said it was a mortal sin, unless you were married.

Even then it could still be a mortal sin, unless you did it with the person you were married to.

And then it was still a mortal sin, unless you did it the right way.

You could burn in hell for sex. So far as I could figure out, watching Johnny Carson wasn't a sin at all. Even nuns stayed up for his monologue.

I listened carefully to Johnny Carson, trying to figure out his mysterious power. Just thinking about what was going on in my neighborhood during his monologue made his jokes spicier.

For weeks, the women giggled over Johnny and Mrs. Mettermann. All you had to do was say his name, and someone would break into snickers.

Then one morning, Mrs. Mettermann came over for coffee. She sat down, and burst out crying.

She was pregnant. Again.

Baby number six.

And she blamed Johnny Carson.

Through the tears and sympathetic noises, all I could hear was she got to laughing during one of Johnny's monologues, and someone—or something—slipped.

"And my youngest goes into the first grade in September," she wailed.

I was old enough to know what that meant. A woman who had all her kids in school full-time was free. She could have the day to herself. She could shop, do serious house cleaning, have a quiet cup of coffee by herself. She could even act like a lady and do a little genteel volunteer work.

Now Mrs. Mettermann was trapped in years of baby business: Washing diapers, sterilizing bottles, lugging diaper bags—not to mention the baby—everywhere she went. She had to go through late-night feedings, teething, potty training and other traumas all over again.

The women sat together in stricken silence.

One thing was for sure, if it was a boy, Mrs. Mettermann wasn't going to call him Johnny.

That night, when my parents turned on Johnny Carson, my father howled at the monologue. But my mother didn't laugh very loud.

I listened to a few jokes, but went to bed before the monologue was over.

What Johnny Carson did to Mrs. Mettermann wasn't funny.

19. The Latin Teacher and the Playboy Bunny

I may be one of the few people outside the priesthood who studied Latin in high school.

Latin, they told us, would build character and discipline. I was a character, all right, but I had no more discipline than any other fifteen year old.

Latin, they said, would give you a base to learn other Romance languages.

Also wrong. After Latin I floundered around in Spanish for years. Today, I couldn't order a taco in a Mexican restaurant. I had no ear for languages. I took Latin for Mr. Henderson's right eyebrow.

Mr. Henderson taught Latin at our Catholic high school. In a desert of nuns and priests, Mr. Henderson was unbearably handsome. He was tall and well-muscled and looked like Sean Connery as James Bond—not that I could ever see one of those evil movies.

He had a way of cocking his right eyebrow that was positively wicked. It made my socks roll down. *Amo, amas, amat* that eyebrow.

The curl that hung down on his forehead like a question-mark wasn't bad, either.

Best of all, Mr. Henderson didn't do any phony flirting. He just talked about his great love, Latin. He sincerely loved that language. I sincerely loved his eyebrow.

It led me through Caesar's long, dull campaigns. *"Gallia est omnis divisa in partes tres. . .* All Gaul is divided into three parts,'' he translated, raising that eyebrow like a bridge. I crossed over it to slog through innumerable accounts of the Romans and their booty. They didn't shake it, they took it.

It didn't matter. I would follow that eyebrow anywhere.

And so went the most curious Latin class in history—row after row of lovesick girls, and a couple of guys who were going to be priests.

It was a situation ripe for trouble. And sure enough, Mr. Henderson got himself into the great Playboy bunny scandal.

It started when we heard Mr. Henderson was engaged. We were shocked. It couldn't be true. That eyebrow couldn't belong to another woman.

Then the rumor spread through school. Mr. Henderson was engaged to marry a Playboy bunny. With blond hair.

If it was true, it was really scandalous. It was a sin just to read *Playboy* magazine. God knows what would happen if you married a real, live bunny. I tried to imagine that eyebrow next to a blond bombshell in a cantilevered bunny suit with a fluffy tail. My eyes crossed.

The debate raged among the students in the cafeteria and the locker area. Was Mr. Henderson committing a sin? Would that eyebrow be twitching in hellfire?

Finally, someone was brave enough to bring it up in religion class. We had debated many great issues during religion. We settled the question of what should you do if you were adrift on the ocean in a lifeboat with three people. Could you eat one to save your life?

The answer was no. That was carrying communion too far. All four had to die.

Personally, I planned to eat the guy and go to confession later. But I felt the chances of this happening in the Midwest were slim. So far, I hadn't even seen a lifeboat, much less an ocean.

So one brave student asked the teacher if it was OK if Mr. Henderson married a Playboy bunny. Without actually saying it, the young inquisitor gave the impression the woman had to be a walking occasion of sin.

The teacher raised both eyebrows at once, something even Mr. Henderson never did. Her eyes bulged. Her lips wiggled around like worms on a hook. She was struggling not to burst into laughter.

She finally said something about what Mr. Henderson did in Holy Matrimony had the blessings of the Church. I can't remember her exact words. They were too painful.

But I knew for sure that Latin was a dead language.

20. It Isn't Easy Being a Saint

My parents grew up on the South Side, the city's old German section. These Germans were a cautious bunch. Their ancestors made one mighty trek across the globe to St. Louis. That seemed to exhaust their wanderlust for generations. Their descendants rarely left the neighborhood. Many moved no more than six blocks from the houses where they were born.

They ran with the same crowd they'd known since grade school, content with the old faces and old ways.

But my parents were restless. They were determined not to raise one more Kraut. So they moved to North County. The relatives carried on as if we'd moved to another country.

We had. Suburbia.

Of course, my parents made this radical move cautiously. In stages. First, they moved out by the airport, about twenty minutes from downtown.

Then, a few years later, they took the big step and bought a home in Florissant, a good forty-five minutes from the city. In the early sixties, Florissant was the end of the world for city people, represented on the maps by clouds and dragons.

Our subdivision was a raw cut in a cornfield with a handful of "Cape Cod" split levels. I think the Cape Cod was in honor of the black shutters the houses sported. They set off the aluminum siding.

The subdivision we moved into was so new, it didn't have a parish yet. The Church was going to have to create a new one. It made us feel important to know that the faraway Church fathers cared about a new parish in Missouri.

We had a priest, but no church. So each Sunday, the newly hatched parish met in a local school gymnasium. As we knelt on the hardwood floor under the scoreboard and basketball net, we felt just like the early Christians.

Every Sunday, we waited for word about what we were going to be called. What was our new parish name? Who was our new saint?

Naturally, we hoped for one of the biggies—the Virgin Mary or one of the Twelve Apostles. But if that didn't work out, we'd settle for one of the more interesting martyrs.

Finally, the great day came. The pastor announced one Sunday that we had our own personal saint.

There was an imposing silence. Not a single folding chair rattled in the gym.

We waited. We got the name. It was:

St. Sabina.

Who?

Nobody had ever heard of her. There were no statues, no holy cards, no prayers to St. Sabina.

Nobody named a kid Sabina.

We didn't know what she looked like, or what she did. We weren't even sure how to pronounce her name. Half the parish insisted she was St. Sabeena.

The parish rumor mill said she was martyred by the Romans by having all her teeth pulled out. That made her the patron saint of dentists. It also ticked off the local dentist, who thought it undid all his preaching about painless dentistry.

We also heard she died a virgin. We weren't surprised. Who'd want her with her teeth out?

The truth was even worse than the rumors.

Somebody had their saints mixed up. It was Apollonia who had her teeth knocked out.

St. Sabina wasn't even a virgin. I had imagined her in white robes, her slender, pale hands holding a lily, like the virgins on the holy cards.

No dice. Sabina was a well-off, devout widow. Now I saw her as a short, shapeless middle-aged woman in a dowdy black dress, with one of those fox furs where the head perpetually bites the tail.

Her story was equally dull. Sabina had been converted by her servant. The servant was martyred first. Sabina followed a month later.

The only other thing we knew was she had a famous church named after her in Rome.

No glamour. No glitz. No word about whether she'd been eaten by lions or consumed by fire. Butler's *Lives of the Saints* simply said Sabina "received her crown a month later."

He made it sound like she'd bought a new hat.

St. Sabina was a terrible disappointment, but we bore it. We put St. Sabina's name on the school soccer and softball uniforms. We pretended we liked the name better than the other parish in Florissant—St. Ferdinand. The Bull.

But I wasn't surprised when St. Sabina got kicked off the liturgical Calendar of Saints, along with St. Christopher and some others.

I remembered that ominous sentence in Butler's *Lives of the Saints*. It said, "But it would seem that we can have no assurance even of the existence of any such martyr."

There we were, a suburban parish in the middle of nowhere, with a saint who may have never existed.

It got worse. Butler concluded: "It remains possible that this was one of the cases in which the founder of a church, whose memory was annually commemorated there, was subsequently mistaken for the patron under whose invocation the church had been built, an appropriate story being invented to do him honor."

If I translated Butler right, that meant all Sabina did was put up the bucks for the church, and gradually she'd been made into a saint.

It made sense. I'd watched the way everyone carried on when old Mr. Vere, the richest man in the parish, came to church. He was the only person, except for a couple of farmers, who didn't live in a subdivision.

He lived on a real, live estate with a ballroom. He wore baggy old clothes and drove a beatup car. Anyone else would have been criticized for looking like that. But people said that's what truly rich people were like. If you had real class, you didn't buy champagne and throw wild parties. You wore old clothes and lived with old furniture and saved your money so your kids could inherit it.

It didn't seem like any fun.

Maybe Sabina was a martyr after all.

21. *Buying Babies*

Whenever I read about unrest in Africa, I get uneasy. I think I may have caused some of it. Not on purpose, of course.

I didn't mean to buy all those pagan babies.

No one uses words like "pagan" any more. But back in the 1950s, when I was buying pagan babies, we didn't know any better.

Actually, I didn't buy whole babies. Just parts. Our class project in my Catholic grade school was saving pagan babies. This was not like saving stamps. We were saving their souls. It cost $5 to baptize a pagan baby for the missions. The whole class donated money to buy a kid.

The Catholic Church has more enlightened programs now. They realize it's easier to save a kid's soul if you feed the body first. But in the fifties, those babies were pagans, and we were snatching them from the fires of hell. For only five bucks.

Our grade-school class had no idea where local babies came from, much less pagan ones. But we always imagined Africa had the best supply. Naturally, pagans would be somewhere in the jungle. Exactly where, we weren't sure. Today's kids aren't the only ones with a hazy knowledge of geography.

Each class had a contest to see how many pagan babies we could save. These were cut-throat competitions. We'd hold bake sales. Wash cars. Give away our milk money. Empty our piggy banks. Even swipe quarters out of our mothers' purses.

We bought those pagan babies by the dozen. It wasn't just the thought of saving their souls that spurred us on.

We got to name the babies.

At home, our parents were having lots of babies, too. But they wouldn't take any of our suggestions for names. Instead they gave our baby brothers and sisters common names like Mark, Michael, or Cathy.

We didn't want ordinary names for our pagan babies. No wimp names, either. We didn't name them after gentle saints who helped the poor and died peacefully in their beds. No, we named our pagan babies after real macho types—saints who died martyrs. And the gorier the death, the better.

That's how some poor kid in Africa got stuck with a name like Emerentiana. We thought it was neat that she was stoned to death while praying at a tomb. It would make a great movie scene, with fake fog and spooky wolf howls.

We rummaged around in the back of our church missals for good saints' names. That's where we found St. Thecla. She was "thrown to wild beasts" by Nero. Not only did she have a dramatic death, but Thecla went out under a glamour name—Nero.

St. Cassian was stuck full of stilettos by his own students. This martyrdom had particular appeal to us.

Who could forget St. Philomena? At age thirteen, she went to Rome. The Emperor Diocletian offered her his hand. And probably other parts, too. She turned him down and was "scourged, thrown into the river, shot full of arrows and finally beheaded." Where else could you get such excitement with a baby for five bucks?

And so it went. We baptized those poor babies and gave each one a gaudy name. We loved it. Then never gave another thought to the ex-pagan kids.

That's why I get a guilty twinge whenever I read about trouble in Africa. Because all those little Philomenas and Emerentianas are grown up now.

And I bet they're mad as hell about being stuck with those names.

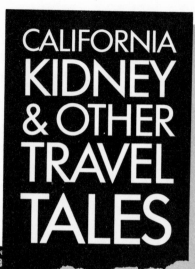

CALIFORNIA
KIDNEY
& OTHER
TRAVEL
TALES

22. The California Kidney and Other Travel Tales

Ever hear of the California kidney?

You won't read anything about it in the guidebooks. But your watch isn't the only thing you have to reset when you travel.

Your kidneys are probably set for your home town.

St. Louis is an easy city to get around in. Everything is about twenty minutes away. The city's kidneys are trained to hold out for a half hour, at the most.

This is no problem when I travel to commuter cities like New York—there are restrooms everywhere.

And in great walking cities, like Chicago, you can always duck into a hotel or restaurant.

But out west, it's another story. Especially in Los Angeles. Once, I was dumb enough to drive from Santa Monica to West Hollywood during rush hour.

About forty-five minutes into the drive, I needed a restroom. So did Don H., the other St. Louisan in the car. We couldn't stop. If we got off the highway, we'd just wander aimlessly through back streets. We didn't see any public restrooms. We couldn't even find a decent bush.

We turned off the radio—those beer commercials were positively painful—and tried to think of deserts. Dry, dusty deserts where the sun beats down and you're thirsty. . . oops, we're back to thinking about water.

We finally made it back to the hotel.

We noticed when we traveled with people who've lived in L.A. for awhile, that they had no problem with the long distances. They'd developed California kidneys. Like camels, they'd solved the problem of water storage.

After water, food is the most serious problem in a strange city. You're in a new city and you have to take some important clients out to dinner. How do you find a good restaurant?

You have reservations, all right—serious ones.

Guidebooks get outdated. Cabbies can be bribed by the big tourist traps. You don't want to wind up at some seafood joint built like a boat that serves $40 fish sticks.

But one method never fails: Call your clients' secretaries. They know their bosses' favorite places. Then make your reservations early.

Never underestimate the power of powerless people, like secretaries, receptionists, janitors.

Or ticket agents at the airport.

That's how the Meek Shall Inherit the Airplane: When bad weather closed the St. Louis airport, I was stranded in Los Angeles—along with about 500 other people. I was at the LAX ticket counter. So was an assertive young man who demanded his rights.

I admired the way he handled himself. He spoke forcefully, even pounded on the counter.

I wimped it. I threw myself on the mercy of the ticket agent. I whimpered. I pleaded. I said I had to get back to work the next morning or I'd be in big trouble. The ticket agent shoehorned me in on a red-eye flight that same night.

The assertive young man got a flight home the next day. I wondered. Was my ticket agent faster? Or had Mr. Assertive's agent stiffed him?

The airlines will deny it, but the people behind the counter say it happens all the time. They reward the nice and punish the nasty. Give them trouble, and you may find yourself on a long, uncomfortable flight home.

Scream that you have to leave now, and you will—and spend the next eighteen hours taking connecting flights.

"I once got stranded in Cedar Rapids," said a woman in the travel industry. "The airport was fogged in. The ticket agents told me to go to my hotel, get a good dinner and a hot bath, and they'd put me on the first flight out in the morning—nothing was leaving the airport that night. The same agents told the jerks they could wait for standby if they wanted. Of course, they did. They sat in the airport for hours, and finally went to their hotel. The hotel dining room was closed. They barely got to sleep before the phones rang with their wakeup calls."

Another agent swears this story is true. Some years back, a Chinese gentleman tried to save money on a flight between China and the West Coast. He bought a tourist-class ticket for himself, and shipped his wife in a trunk with airholes.

"The poor woman died horribly," said the agent. "The compartment for animals is pressurized, but the luggage compartment isn't."

Remember: When you ship relatives, put them in pet caddies.

23. Hollywood Christmas

It was Christmas Day, and Don H. and I were walking down Hollywood Boulevard. We'd run away from home for the holidays, away from the polite parties and the endless dinners. We wanted some place that had never heard of Christmas. Hollywood, of course. So we ran away to Los Angeles.

We stayed in a great old hotel, the Chateau Marmont in West Hollywood. The lobby was straight out of a Gloria Swanson movie: castle-sized furniture, dark old paintings, and lacy wrought iron in the lobby arches. We had a slightly seedy suite with a spectacular view of L.A. for $160 a day. I never got tired of that view. At night, the lights twinkled all over the city, brownish orange, silver white, and blue. In the morning, the smog-dusted sunrise glowed pink and yellow.

We heard that Robert De Niro stayed at the Chateau Marmont. We knew that John Belushi died there, in a poolside cabana.

Everyone at the Marmont except for us seemed to be in the movie business. The night clerks all looked like undiscovered actors.

A French filmmaker used to eat in the coffee shop and argue with his entourage. The only word I could understand—even when he spoke English—was ''montage.''

A young woman who sounded like the bubbleheaded Boopsie in Doonesbury was talking to a young man in jeans and a bomber jacket about a video she was working on. She was explaining the plot to him.

''So we kidnap this yuppie,'' she said, in her spacy, little girl voice. ''And we really blow his mind. We don't hurt him, you know. We just expand his horizons. He meets this girl on the beach . . . .''

We rented a car that the rental agency called a classic. It was actually a red 1965 Buick Skylark convertible, with the original leather seats and a bad new paint job. It also had the original 1965 brakes, which didn't stop the car unless you stood on them.

But as long as we drove along without thinking about how some day we might have to stop it, the car was fast and fun. We zipped along the beach with the top down and the radio on, blasting Beach Boys music from a nostalgia station.

At first, we thought the convertible had a leaky muffler. It smelled of car exhaust. Then we rolled down the windows, and the smell got worse. That wasn't a leaky muffler. It was the Los Angeles air. People breathe that stuff.

Never mind. We loved L.A. We'd inhale when we got back home.

Meanwhile, we saw Forest Lawn. We took the Universal Studios tour. And on Christmas Day, we were on Hollywood Boulevard, making the Walk of Stars. We stopped to read each famous name at our feet: Bing Crosby, Lawrence Welk, Alfred Hitchcock, Judy Canova. Whatever happened to Judy Canova?

We stopped to watch the ''living mannequin'' outside the wax museum. The mannequin, a fiftyish guy in an emcee's tux, moved to the music with the jerky dignity of a robot. Then the tape stopped and he stepped off the platform and smiled. The crowd burst into shocked applause.

He was superb. But we spotted him as human just before he finished his routine. Robots don't have a slight sag around the jawline.

At Frederick's of Hollywood, we looked in the windows and marvelled at the sleazy black and red underwear and the impossibly high hooker heels.

A block or two later, we saw a real hooker.

She was standing on the street corner in a way that announced her profession better than any red light. She carried a big, soft black leather purse, the kind that New York women wear under their armpits.

She was beautiful. That doesn't mean much in L.A., where every waitress and counter clerk was beautiful. But she had gorgeous cheekbones, and the kind of bony face that cameras make love to. She seemed to be in her late twenties.

She was very tall. She had to stoop slightly to talk to a short, toadlike man in a brown leather coat that looked like it was cut from cardboard.

She wore a straight skirt, a long-sleeved sweater, and spindly hooker heels. The same ones we'd seen in the window at Frederick's.

Her skin was unusually pale. Her hair was long, straight, and light brown. She stopped talking to the toad and he moved away. She straightened up and I saw that her eyes were . . . red.

Not bloodshot. Not hungover. The whites were bright red. If she didn't close her eyes she might bleed to death.

"She doesn't look healthy," said Don H. "I wonder what's wrong with her?"

Just then a red rustbucket convertible from the early seventies pulled up at her corner. Inside was a curly-haired man whose muscles were turning to fat. He was clearly someone she knew. She climbed into the car, hiking her tight skirt to get in.

That's when we saw them: the needlemarks on the backs of her legs, right at her knees. They were in two rows, as neat as purple thumbtacks.

Now I thought I understood the pale skin and bleeding red eyes. She was a junkie. It was ten o'clock in the morning, and she may have been working all night without success. Christmas Eve isn't a good time for customers. She was tired and needed a fix.

I shuddered.

Only Hollywood would have a scene so corny: A junkie hooker on Christmas Day.

24. What Those Travel Cliches Really Say

I knew I was an official travel writer when I caught myself actually saying "palm-fringed beaches." I didn't mean to talk that way. I couldn't help myself.

Travel writing breeds cliches the way a wet basement breeds water-bugs. They're just as ugly. And you'll never kill them off completely.

When you think you've exterminated all those pesky "palm-fringed beaches" you find your copy is crawling with "friendly natives." That means they won't pick your pocket at the airport.

On the other hand, when you deliver a little lecture on "Third World poverty" and advise everyone to "leave your watch and jewelry at home and wear a money belt," that means the colorful local folks will steal the fillings out of your teeth. Or, to be exact, rip your pierced earrings right out of your ears.

That actually happened to a woman touring Peru. The people traveling with her considered the incident her fault. She shouldn't have flaunted her American wealth.

But if she'd read the tourist brochures and guidebooks, she would have known what to expect. The old dependable cliches would have warned her, without actually saying anything so upsetting she'd cancel her trip.

Travel writing is an artful code. Here's a partial translation of common phrases from brochures and guidebooks:

The Viets Guide to Travel Cliches

An old inn furnished with antiques: The bed squeaks and the radiator rattles all night.

Children stay free with parents: Mom and Dad live like brother and sister.

Look for that sign of salvation in the brochure: "Free children's programs." That means Mom and Dad get a chance to be alone while the kids play with modeling clay.

Easy-going, relaxed pace: It takes room service three hours to deliver breakfast in your $200 a day room. Nothing runs all night but the toilet. And the smiling housekeeping staff keeps promising to bring the towels, but never gets around to it.

Elegant hotel: Expensive and stuffy. Don't wear your swimsuit in the lobby.

Elegant restaurant: Waiters in tuxes serve overpriced pasta.

Escape the hectic pace of everyday life: There's nothing to do.

Everyone gathers to watch the tropical sunset: And get drunk.

Hands-on museum: Even YOUR kids can't break anything. Also, educational, well-meaning and probably dull.

Largest in North America: This (park, log cabin, school, skyscraper) is so dull I can't think of anything else to say.

See also "Oldest West of the Mississippi."

Luxury hotel: Overpriced.

No-nonsense affordable accomodations: The towels are the size of washcloths and the sheets pull off the bed in the middle of the night.

Our island has all the modern conveniences: There's a McDonald's and a Kentucky Fried.

Our island is unspoiled: You'd better like fish.

Tastefully decorated hotel rooms: Done in pastels. Also, the pictures aren't bolted to the wall.

25. The Man Who Flew a Million Miles

In six years, Joe Perez flew almost a million miles on business. That's more than four trips to the moon. But Joe wasn't crammed into a capsule and fed freeze-dried food. He went first class all the way. He even flew the supersonic Concorde.

Ah, but don't envy Joe too much for his high life. He traveled most of those miles in disguise. He dressed as the most despised of all travelers: the tourist.

That's right. The polyester guy on the package tour, with all those cameras around his neck. The person who relies on his Fodor's to tell him where everyone goes. The person who winds up in the recommended native bar or restaurant, looking at a lot of other people from Akron or Omaha, and thinking he's seeing real life.

But tourists don't travel on the Concorde, you say.

Sure they do. Maybe they sold the farm. Or made a nice bundle with that factory in Springfield.

Now they want some glamour. They want to see the world. The world sees only their money. The poor tourist is practically invisible.

And that's the way Joe liked it.

Because Joe was a prime terrorist target—a salesman for a large international corporation. In the early eighties, his job took him all over the world: Singapore, Arabia, Europe, and Africa. And lots of New York-to-London flights on the Concorde.

Some of those places were hot spots for terrorism. And a rich American businessman is a big target. But he's also faceless and interchangeable. Consider what would happen if Joe got blown away on a trip: There would be angry protests from the U.S. government. A couple of editorials. Promises of an inquiry by the country where the awful act occurred. And in about a week, Joe would be forgotten, except by his grieving family.

On the other hand, if the terrorists blew up somebody famous, like Mother Teresa or Michael Jackson, you'd never hear the end of it. The evildoers would be hunted to the ends of the earth.

That's why Joe had to make himself invisible.

"Everyone on the Concorde gets dressed up in furs and jewels," he said. "That's too noticeable. Too dangerous. Don't attract any attention if you're traveling abroad. I dressed casual, low-key. I wore no business suit, no jewelry, nothing expensive. In customs, I said I was a tourist."

The Concorde attracts big money, big celebrities and big business. Business executives fly on the Concorde because they won't get jet lag. The Concorde takes three hours and forty minutes to go from New York to London. A regular flight takes almost seven hours.

Concorde airfare is about $7,000 roundtrip. That's the price of a small car. But it's not much to pay when a big corporation is negotiating a multi-million-dollar deal and they need an alert executive. Jet lag can cripple you for three days or more.

"The British are known to take advantage of business people with jet lag," Joe said. "So are the Orientals and the Arabs. In fact, they all do it."

They're too slick to ask you to their offices.

"They want to take you out for a night on the town. Before you know it, they're talking business, and your mind is halfway across the ocean."

So now we have Joe, dressed for his own brand of success in ordinary clothes, on his way to the Concorde lounge at Heathrow airport in London.

"I liked to get there early for the champagne and hors d'oeuvres," Joe said. Then he settled into a soft leather couch, and waited in champagne-cushioned comfort. But what came into the lounge nearly made him drop his caviar.

"I looked over and who did I see but Henry the K, Henry Kissinger. Everyone wanted to shake his hand. Not me.

"It was a rather full flight, and every seat in the lounge was taken except a bench behind my couch. It was covered in leather, but it's still a bench. I had my arm stretched out on the back of the couch, Kissinger had his arm propped up and there I was, literally rubbing elbows with Henry the K."

Joe was not thrilled.

"This was 1985, around the time of the Frankfort airport bombing. Kissinger is a very recognizable figure, and nobody knows who I am. I thought to myself: If he gets blown away, it doesn't take much for a bullet to go through a leather couch.

"So I got up, went over to the end of the room and stood by the bar. And I waited until everyone boarded before I got on. You don't want to hang around a well-known figure when you travel."

Joe isn't the only invisible tourist.

"On one Concorde flight, the guy next to me was dressed in clothes even older than mine. Plus he had a two-day growth of beard. I figured this bum really had to be interesting.

"Sure enough, it turned out he was a high official in an international brokerage firm. Head of the whole Far East division. Here's a guy making two mil a year and he's dressed worse than I was."

The next time you fly in luxury, forget the flashy dressers and the obvious celebrities. You can read about them in the checkout line at the supermarket.

Look for the person who looks like no one.

There's a real first-class story.

26. How to Save at the Airport

Some people have a miserable time when they're stuck in an airport. Some get bored and spend too much money.

Not me.

I got stranded in the Los Angeles International Airport for 14 hours, and managed to save $298.26.

Here is my amazing story:

One Christmas, Don H. and I went to California to research the effects of sunshine on Midwestern skin. We were going to take a leisurely 11 A.M. flight back to St. Louis.

We arrived at the airport early, stood in line for an hour, and found out our flight was canceled. So was the next flight. And the next one. The St. Louis airport was closed by bad weather. We couldn't catch a flight out until 1:03 A.M.

Don H. and I reconnoitered the nearest airport bar, ordered two drinks, and thought about what we were going to do for the next fourteen hours.

The cab ride to our hotel was $30 one-way—so it would cost a small fortune to go back there.

It was pretty expensive sitting around and drinking, too. The two drinks cost $5.82 and we polished them off in ten minutes. At that rate, we would drink $488.88 by the time our 1:03 flight rolled around.

Many other passengers simply gave up, and prepared to eat molten plastic and doze on airport benches for the next fourteen miserable hours. But Don H. and I had an inspiration. We remembered that even respectable airport hotels rented rooms by the hour, or had short day rates.

We would get a comfortable hotel room, take a shower, take a nap, take it easy.

Sure enough, the Hyatt at Los Angeles Airport would take us. We explained our problem on the phone to the reservations person. She said we could have a room for $50 until our flight took off. It was cheap comfort at $25 a person. Better yet, the hotel shuttle bus would pick us up absolutely free. Another savings.

At the hotel, the clerk said, "I'm sorry I can't give you the room for $50. You'll be checking out after 7 P.M."

"But the reservations person promised," said Don H.

"We have no record of that," said the clerk.

Don H. raised one eyebrow. The signal. Cops aren't the only ones who play good-guy, bad-guy.

I never raised my voice. I just hardened it, and fixed the clerk with a glare. "She promised," I said.

He gave a little rabbity gulp and said, "You can have the room at the $50 rate."

We felt so good winning this bargain, we went off to the coffee shop for lunch. A $39 lunch. That seemed pricey for fish and an omelet, but food isn't cheap any more.

Besides, by now we would have drunk $69.84 at the airport bar, so we were still saving money.

Next, we took a long walk in the California sun. Then we returned to the room and discovered the robo bar. This was a neat little invention. Pull out a tiny bottle, and it triggered a computer signal in the front desk's cash register. We had that sucker ringing to the tune of $13.34 for four doll-sized drinks. But it was now 7 P.M., and we would have drunk $279.36 in the airport bar.

We would have had to eat airport hot dogs, too. When our hotel had such a good restaurant. We decided to treat ourselves to a nice dinner. The chicken and prime rib came to $74.52. That seemed a little steep. But it was almost 10 P.M. We would have downed $384.12 in the airport bar.

Soon it was time to check out. The clerk started to say, "I can't charge you the $50 rate because it's after 7 o'clock," but we froze him with one look.

In less than fourteen hours, we'd managed to spend $190.62 at the airport hotel, including dinner, phone calls, tariffs on the phone calls, taxes, and the robo bar.

We still felt ourselves blessed. If we'd been drinking in the airport bar for 14 hours, we would have spent $488.88. And the tip would have been a whopper.

We took the Hyatt's free shuttle bus back to the airport, and boarded the plane, pleased with all the money we'd managed to save.

The airline saved us even more money. When we landed, we didn't have to pay a porter to carry our bags.

The airline lost our luggage.

27. *Speedy Justice*

It was a rare warm day in late winter. I had a rare day off work, and rarest of all, I was driving a red Jaguar. Now I was tearing down I-55. The car ripped along the gray highway like a razor through silver silk. In less than an hour we were at Litchfield, Ill., 50 miles from St. Louis. We'd be in Chicago by suppertime.

The Jag was Don H.'s dream car. He rarely let anyone else sit in his car, much less drive it. But he trusted me to take it to Chicago. Maybe it's because I have an honest face. Maybe it's because we've been married eighteen years.

Don H. popped in a new Buddy Holly tape. It was the drum solo from "Peggy Sue." I don't know if you've ever heard it, but that pounding drum sets the blood racing. I cranked up the volume. Then I cranked up the car. Then I saw the Illinois highway patrol car.

But not before he saw me. He was on the other side of the divided highway. I thought that made me out of season. But he pulled a U-turn across two lanes of oncoming traffic, crossed the median strip and pulled me over.

"I clocked you at 89," the officer said. "Your driver's license, ma'am."

I was calm. I reached in my wallet and handed him my credit card. He handed it back. It was over the limit, too.

The officer's name was Savage. But he didn't look it. He looked young. Even younger than the doctors look these days. This means I am a taxpayer and semi-respectable citizen. But I can't help it. I grew up in the sixties. Whenever I see anything with a badge and a uniform, I break out in a cold sweat, and want to flush everything in my purse down the toilet.

The officer told me to follow him back to patrol headquarters. On the way, Don H. offered this advice: "Pretend he's a 900-pound gorilla. No matter what he says, tell him 'Yes, sir.' "

"Are you the newspaper columnist?" the officer said.

Yes, sir. That's me. The fastest columnist in St. Louis.

"I don't meet many celebrities," he said. "I'm scared."

I don't feel too good, either.

"You know I can't let you off," he said.

I'm not asking for any favors, I said. I remembered that line from a forties prison movie. I thought it sounded cool.

"You'll have to post bail," the officer said. "It's $70 cash."

I opened my wallet and everything fell out on the floor. Including three $1 bills. That was all the cash I had with me. Don H. posted bail with his vacation money. "I give good bond," he said.

I'm going to fight it, I told him later.

"But you're guilty," said Don H.

Guilty people get off all the time for crimes like murder and robbery. Remember the guy who killed the San Francisco mayor? He got off with voluntary manslaughter because he ate junk food. Called it the Twinkie Defense.

I'd had a blameless record for twenty years. Then, suddenly, I got caught going an insane speed. It wasn't my fault. I was driven crazy by the Buddy Holly drum solo. I had the Drum Defense.

My friends were unsympathetic. "You're just one of those jerks who passes me on the highway," said one.

The Drum Defense also failed to impress my attorney. He said we had a real hanging judge. The best I could hope for was parole. I would pay a fat fine and be released under the supervision of the court for three months.

The red brick courthouse was in Hillsboro. It had a neon sign that said, "The World Needs God."

"Oh, Lord," said the lawyer. I think he read it as "All Hope Abandon, Ye Who Enter Here."

The lawyer tried. He told the judge this ticket would put one whopping zit on my unblemished record. He said it would raise my insurance. The judge said he could make no exceptions.

Then the lawyer said the same thing all over again. So did the judge.

Then I pleaded guilty. "I'm sorry," the lawyer said.

Me, too. If I'd been arrested for murder, you might have had something to work with.

28. A Guide to Gracious Train Travel

Gracious train travel has been nearly forgotten. It's hard to feel gracious when your train has been sitting on a siding outside Cleveland for six hours.

But these stories are becoming part of the bad old days. Certain runs are so improved, they're almost up to 1930s standards. Passengers with suits are beginning to outnumber persons with cardboard suitcases. Train travel is almost respectable.

This **Guide To Gracious Train Travel** is based on one round-trip from St. Louis to Chicago.

The Announcement: As soon as you announce you're going by train, your friends will say it takes too long. You could spend hours arguing. It may become difficult to remain gracious.

Actually, trains are just as fast as planes when you're going to Chicago. Here is a scientific breakdown:

Train time—6 hours

Flying time—6 hours

The flying-time figure includes:

One hour at the St. Louis airport's cocktail lounge, getting the courage to fly.

One hour actual flying time to O'Hare in Chicago.

One hour circling O'Hare, waiting to land.

One hour locating your luggage.

One hour to find a taxi and drive into Chicago.

One hour to sober up, after the courage you got in St. Louis.

You will also have to listen to train horror stories from your friends. Five years ago, on a trip to Chicago, the roadbed washed out and the passengers were herded into buses and driven along country roads for hours. In the army, or in college, they were packed into cattle cars and they swore they'd never take a train again. A St. Louis-bound Amtrak train derailed outside Springfield two weeks ago.

Graciously counter these tales with airplane horror stories, perhaps how you got marooned in the Little Rock airport on Christmas Eve. If that fails, remind them what happened to Buddy Holly, The Big Bopper, Jim Croce and Lynyrd Skynyrd at the peak of their careers. That should do it.

The Ticket: The Amtrak reservation system is the equal of any airline's. You hang on the phone, and listen to a taped apology played over and over. Finally, a ticket agent comes on the line. Round-trip coach fare is $45.50.

The agent recited the train times to Chicago. I took one called the State House. It left St. Louis at 4:30 in the morning and got in at 10:25 A.M.

The Departure: The eleven-year-old temporary Amtrak station is in a weed patch under an overpass downtown. It looks like a construction trailer. But there are advantages.

First, you don't have to go through security.

Second, there are no shuttle buses for long-term parking. There isn't much parking, period, long-term or short-term.

I recognized the passengers from the old days: A white youth. A black youth. A young woman with a squalling child. An extremely crabby old gentleman and his long-suffering wife. She kept trying to placate the old fellow. He kept yelling, "Shut up!"

The train boarded promptly at 4:15. Skilled travelers will debate the merits of smoking vs. non-smoking cars. Non-smoking sections attract young mothers with kids who lie in the aisles and scream. Smoking sections attract muscular young persons carrying radios bigger than their suitcases. Always take the non-smoking car. It's safer to glare at little kids than big ones.

Female business persons will prefer the train. Many of the conductors are young men with mustaches. They are easier on the eyes than skinny young flight attendants.

Once you have selected the car, choose your seat. Make sure you have one by a window. Train seats are about like airplane seats, except there are only two on each side of the aisle, so you have more room. If you pile your coat and books in the seat next to you, you may get both seats to yourself. If someone comes near you, glare and sigh loudly. You can also talk quietly to yourself. Or read texts aloud from the Bible. This will ensure that you sit alone, even on a crowded train.

29. Calling the Coast

If you're in an office in the Midwest, you may go through the daily ritual known as "calling the coast."

That's the East Coast and the West Coast. By "East Coast" I mean New York. There are other cities along the Atlantic Seaboard, but New York doesn't know that. Besides, office workers in Boston and Philadelphia act just like people anywhere.

The West Coast is California, especially Los Angeles. Oregon and Washington may be on the coast, but you'd never know it to talk to them.

You live in what the coasts call the Flyover—that vast, unexplored area they fly over to get from one coast to the other. No one from either coast will admit to actually visiting the Flyover. But they hear rumors it is populated by backward people who wear last year's fashions.

The reason you have to take special care to call the coasts is they are in another time zone—and another consciousness.

Mornings in Midwest offices are spent calling the East Coast. You'll find New Yorkers in their offices about 10 A.M., New York time. The best time to reach them is between 10 and noon. At 12 sharp, the whole city goes to lunch for two hours, and complains that all the restaurants are crowded. After 2 P.M., New Yorkers disappear for the rest of the day.

Don't waste your time making small talk about the weather. New Yorkers rarely encounter any as they go from building to building. The only weather that has any effect is rain. It makes all the cabs disappear.

Manhattan has its own brand of polite conversation. New Yorkers like to talk about how busy they are. It is polite for a New Yorker to cut short any conversation with you by saying, "Well, I'm busy. Gotta run."

It is not polite for you to be busy. You live in the Midwest, where nothing happens.

During a business call, New Yorkers may also complain about traffic snarls and muggings. It is impolite to say you are sorry. But the real faux pas is to tell them what a nice city you live in. Talking about hardships is how New Yorkers brag. They know only a superior person could survive life in the big city jungle. Wimps live in pleasant places.

If you live in the Midwest, you don't have all the cultural advantages of someone who works in Manhattan. Nevermind that they couldn't afford a Broadway theater ticket and haven't had time to go to a gallery in years. It's there if they want it.

Besides, you can't get good pastrami in the Midwest.

While New York is at lunch, you might want to eat too. That way, you'll get back to your office around 1 o'clock, just in time for the West Coast lunch hour.

Remember, the West Coast is three hours away from New York— three hours behind the time. In other words, they're a little bit slow. This is called "laid back." Even if they're busy, they won't sound like it.

Californians love to talk about the weather. This is the West Coast way of bragging.

A typical California conversation goes like this: "How's the weather in St. Louis?"

The correct answer is, "Lousy."

Then they get to tell you it's 70 degrees, and they're going to sit around the pool after work.

Occasionally, your city will have a rare nice day. There's only one way to get out of this embarrassing situation: Apologize, and tell them you now have some idea what it's like to live in California.

30. A Negative View of Vacation Pictures

I've finally found a way to shock my friends. It isn't sex, drugs or drink.

It's photographs. No, I don't have negatives on anyone. In fact, I don't have any negatives at all.

The whole thing started when I told a man I was going on vacation. He was the first to react this way, but not the last.

"Are you going to take pictures on your vacation?" he asked.

No. I don't have a camera. I'm a terrible photographer.

"No camera," he said. He couldn't have been more shocked if I said I lived in a shack with no indoor plumbing.

"Everyone has a camera," he said. "Can I loan you mine?"

No. Then you'd have to see my vacation pictures. And they would send you screaming from the room.

I thought I was being responsible. Most people are lousy photographers, but they take vacation pictures anyway. Then they unleash the misbegotten things on the rest of us. I believe not owning a camera is like having your pet spayed. I don't let unwanted animals proliferate,

and I don't bring unwanted photographs into the world.

No one likes looking at home-made vacation pictures. They're always blurry beige and gray, with a patch of green. The beige and gray are buildings. The green is grass. Unless it's ocean.

In the hands of an amateur photographer, a castle in Spain looks about like a souvenir stand at Silver Dollar City. The only things that ever turn out right are the palm trees. And if you've seen one palm tree, you've seen them all.

Besides, I don't want to remember what's standing in front of the palm tree. It's usually a couple of blue people. Then I could say, "That's Frank and Edith on the beach in their down jackets. The island was having the worst cold spell in twenty-five years."

To head off the audience's snickers, I'd add defensively, "It was still warmer than the Midwest."

I don't want a photo of that delightful couple, Frank and Edith, who I met on vacation, either. They live in my memory as funny and warm-hearted. When I see the photograph I remember that Edith's false teeth clicked, and Frank had a mustard-colored leisure suit.

I also don't want any photos of me. I remember myself as witty and relaxed. It's only when I look at the photos that I see just how relaxed I was. I look like a coconut dropped on my head. Maybe it has something to do with all those pina coladas.

I prefer my colorful memories. I'd rather tell you about my luxurious vacation hotel than show you one more Holiday Inn. I'd rather tell you I dressed casually than show you a photo of me in clothes that spent a week stuffed in a suitcase.

Some people say, "But memories fade. Don't you want something lasting, so you can look back months later and remember all the places you went?"

I have it.

Each month, I get my credit card bill.

ACTING LIKE ANIMALS

31. The Drug-Sniffing Cat

Dogs are so straight. No wonder politicians pose with them to look respectable. You won't catch them with a kinky cat for their campaigns.

Dogs even get jobs. There are seeing-eye dogs for the blind. Drug-sniffing dogs work for the cops.

Drug-sniffing cats are another story. I have one. I don't think the cops would want her. The little freak loves the stuff.

The cat's name is Elsah. We called her that because we found the calico cat in the middle of the highway near the town of Elsah, Ill. A few miles down the road, and she would have been called Wood River.

Elsah the cat started on her life of shame and degradation because of a houseguest. The houseguest said he was short of funds. We soon found out what he was spending his money on.

Late one Saturday night, we heard a thump from his room upstairs. Elsah came rolling down the steps, zig-zagged back to our bedroom, jumped up, and skidded across the bedside table, taking the lamp with her. She landed on her back, with a goofy look on her face. The houseguest came down, looking even goofier. "Elsah loves pot," he said, giggling. "She even sleeps on my stash."

Sure enough, Elsah had made it back up the steps and was curled up on a large baggie filled with dried green leaves that I don't think came out of a spice rack.

"I just blow the smoke in her face," the houseguest said. "She loves it."

It turned out the houseguest had been entertaining himself with large quantities of leaves, seeds, pills, and powders. Plus some curious animal tranquilizers he got from a friendly vet.

God only knows what else he'd tried on Elsah. Don H. offered to realign his spine if he ever came near the cat again. That must have made him feel unwelcome. The next day, we saw the garden hose dangling from his third-story window, and knew he'd left abruptly, along with his waterbed.

After his departure, Elsah paced the house restlessly. We thought she'd forget him.

Then we had the house redone, and we found Elsah throwing herself at the painter. She followed him everywhere. Especially down to the basement, where she sat by the hour, inhaling paint thinner. When the painter poured it down the drain, she even sat by that, sniffing the fumes.

"That stuff's not good for her, lady," said the painter. "It's addictive."

We knew that. We also knew why she followed the exterminator on his rounds, when he sprayed our house with those interesting chemicals.

"I don't understand it," said the man. "Most animals hate the stuff. But she can't stay away from it."

She wouldn't stay away from any of the scuzzier types who came to the house, either. Normally, Elsah was picky about people. She turned up her nose at genteel guests who called, "Here, kitty, kitty." She ignored kindly repair people who tried to pet her. She sized you up for several visits before she came out to make friends.

But when we had a rented TV delivered by a guy who looked like a member of the Manson family, Elsah threw herself at him. The TV guy kicked her away, but Elsah ran back. She looked like a rich girl chasing a carny barker.

We could guess what the attraction was. His clothes had a rich, autumnal smell like burning leaves—and it was July.

Oh, the howls we heard when we locked her away from her current candy man. Elsah would throw herself at the locked door, trying to get at him. The men always wondered what the attraction was. We knew they had a certain air about them.

On a friend's first visit to our house, Elsah crawled into the guy's lap and rolled around joyously, while he looked puzzled.

After he left, Don H. said, "I didn't know Jim used drugs. You sure can't tell."

But Elsah could.

We even tried the cat version of methadone. We bought her a little catnip, because we'd heard it was similar to marijuana.

But Elsah wouldn't touch the stuff. After what she'd had, catnip had the same kick as oregano.

It's been ten years since the houseguest introduced Elsah to drugs, and except for her fling with the painter, we've kept her away from the stuff ever since. But when people tell me cats are clean animals, I figure they're dopes.

32. *Hairy Problems*

I call it the Case of the Sprayed Sister. You could say it was one of Linda Poor's hairiest problems.

But all Linda's problems are hairy. She's a cat behaviorist at Kennelwood Village, which boards and trains dogs and cats. She's sort of a cat shrink. Her specialty is hopeless cases. Cat owners from St. Louis to Washington consult her.

In the Sprayed Sister case, the family cat was zapping a nun. "This was serious," Linda said. "The nun came to visit the family. Every time she showed up, the cat sprayed her. The family wanted it stopped."

It turned out to have nothing to do with the nun. "When the good sister came to the door, the cat saw another cat in the yard. The cat began marking its territory—which included the nun."

The Phantom Rival was another territory case. "A woman had two four-year-old male cats. From the age of six weeks, one would spray around the edges of the living room and dining room. When she moved to a new apartment, it stopped for awhile, then started up again. Why?

"Finally, it hit me. The mirrors! She had floor-to-ceiling mirrors in the dining room. I asked, 'How long did it stop after the move?' She said, 'A week.'

" 'Did you put up the mirrors when you moved in, or did you wait?' " She waited a week.

"I said the problem would go away if she took down the mirrors. She tried an experiment first. She taped newspapers over the mirrors. The spraying stopped immediately. The cat was seeing itself in the mirrors, and marking its territory against a rival."

Linda saved several cats on their way to the Big Sleep. One was a lively little "domestic short hair." That's a polite term for alley cat.

"The owner said it was aggressive. That was her interpretation, not mine. When the cat was adopted it had a broken hip. It wore a plaster cast, so it was very quiet. Then the cast came off and it was BOING! BOING! all over the house. It chased Mickey, the old cat. Mickey would climb up on the furniture to get away. The new cat still wasn't much of a climber because of its bad hip.

"The owner thought Mickey was being bullied. Worse, the young cat was attacking the woman. She was undergoing chemotherapy and couldn't risk scratches and bites. She was afraid the young cat would have to go.

"There were several problems going on at once. First, the cat was probably taken away from its mother too young. It never learned to play properly. I wondered, because it came to the shelter with a broken hip, if someone hadn't been playing too rough with it. That can happen with kittens.

"Mickey, the older cat, would tolerate this rough play as long as it could. There would be fierce cat fights, and Mickey would box its ears. It was teaching it to play. When Mickey got tired of the young cat, it would climb up on something to get away. Mickey was handling the situation just fine.

"I told the owner not to interfere. If she thought the fights were too

fierce, she should say, 'Both of you stop it!' and not single out the young cat.''

The owner helped trigger the cat's "aggression," although she didn't realize it.

She was petting her cat too much.

"The cat was getting turned on. Too much petting can be over-stimulating. Then it bites.

"I had her count the pats. Twelve was the cat's limit. There are other ways to love your cat. She could give it love pats with her voice.

"The cat calmed down in three weeks."

Linda handled another doomed cat with a phone call or two.

"The woman and her husband were partially sighted—and great animal lovers. They had seeing-eye dogs, plus several pet dogs and cats. She had rescued a white domestic short hair. The new cat wouldn't come when she called, or answer to its name. I asked if it was deaf—some white cats are—but she said, no, she'd had it checked.

"Because the woman was almost blind, she needed to know where the cat was. So she put a bell on its collar. Now she knew where it was—but so did all the other cats. This was the new kid on the block. It couldn't get any privacy.

"First, I had her take the bell off.

"Then, I told her this cat needed extra love and couldn't ask for it. She should pick it up, pet it and love it.

"After awhile, the cat became very responsive. It purred, asked to be petted, knew its name, and answered when she called. And she was about to have it put to sleep!

"What we call bad behavior is a cat trying to tell us something," Linda said. "We are supposed to be intellectual beings. We should try to under-stand what the cat's saying."

Some problems can be solved if you look at them from the cat's point of view. Like this case: A couple in their eighties were puzzled when their well-behaved cat suddenly quit using the litter box. They couldn't understand what was wrong. They kept the box clean and used plastic liners.

Linda immediately suspected the liners.

"I don't like them, and cats don't, either," she said. "I suggested they take the liners out."

It worked. "They told me the cat had used liners for awhile, and I believed them. But all it takes is one bad experience—the liner catches a claw, or bunches up—and the cat won't use the box again."

If you have a cat problem, Linda hopes you won't consult her first. "It could be a physical problem. Take your cat to the vet and have it checked. If you're willing to spend money on me, spend it on the vet first."

She makes house calls. Those are $45. Linda charges $30 for an hour at the office, $15 for half an hour on the phone.

Some methods are harder on the owner than the cat. One is confinement, a common cure for litter box problems. Confinement works this way: You keep the cat in a small, uncarpeted room for seven days. A half-bath is ideal. Fix it up as comfortably as possible with the cat's favorite toys, blanket, food, water and most important, a clean litter box.

"This is not punishment. It's a way to retrain the cat. But owners have a hard time believing that.

"You must take out your cat often, pet it and play with it. During and after confinement, you need to give the cat lots of attention. Just don't allow it to wander anywhere unsupervised."

It may take four to six weeks of concentrated effort to cure the cat. One case took a whole year.

"This lady dearly loved her cat. It was an intelligent, even-tempered animal. She could take it out on a leash. It went camping with the family. Then, all of a sudden, it started using her son's room. Just before it struck, the cat would scream and run around like it was on fire.

"We had the cat checked by a vet. We looked at changes in feeding schedules. And the fact that her husband was away on business.

"I suggested she crate the cat in its pet caddy in the morning, two or three hours before it went into its screaming routine, then uncrate it in the bathroom where it had its litter box. Finally, the cat began using its litter box again, but the woman still had to crate it first.

"Then she told me, just by coincidence, that the problem started when she began babysitting an infant in her home. When she stopped, so did the cat. It was jealous. It didn't like that baby.

"Not all cats are like that. Some are very fond of babies. If you're worried about trouble with the cat when you bring home the baby, you can do things to make the situation easier. It depends on the new mother and how much time she has.

"While she and the baby are still in the hospital, she can send home a diaper that's been sprinkled on, possibly a bib with a little milk on it or some talcum powder. Let the cat know these new smells.

"If the cat is attached to the wife, let the husband walk in the house with the new baby the first time.

"And don't get hyper if you see the cat around the baby. It's an old wives' tale that cats like to suck the breath out of infants. They're attracted by the milk smell. Still, you must protect the sleeping environment of a very young baby. Cats may curl up with a baby to get warm, and when a cat weighs ten or fifteen pounds, it could smother a small baby.

"Call the cat over to sit by the nursing mother. Nursing is pleasant, and cats pick up those vibrations. They are very sensitive."

Cats are also sensitive to unpleasantness. Linda once had a case where the father threatened to do away with the cat unless it quit using the floor. Linda didn't care for the father. Neither did the cat.

She recommended confinement. It seemed to work. Then the problem started up again.

"The cat was very attached to the pre-teen daughter. When I went back, I didn't see the girl all night, and the mother seemed unusually nervous. Finally, I took her aside and said, 'What's going on here?'

"The mother said the daughter was in a drug treatment hospital. The cat started using the floor the day she went into the hospital. It was very sensitive to what was happening in that house."

33. The Deer Hunter

The deer hunter is a wild tale that's been heard everywhere from Scotland Yard to the White House. I first heard it from a St. Louis teacher, Kay Boyce. She thought the story was an urban legend. It went something like this:

A hunter hit a deer with his car. He put the illegal deer in the back seat. The animal came back to life. The man tried to hit the deer with a tire iron, but hit his dog instead. The dog bit the man. The man ran for a pay phone and called the police.

Kay said, "I understand the officer on duty has a tape and is making copies for all his friends, but I don't know if it's a city or county cop."

After that column, I got more than twenty-five calls from people who had the tape. I wound up with three copies. The first one came from Thomas A. Villa, president of the St. Louis Board of Aldermen.

That deer tape had entertained everyone from the mayor of St. Louis to members of the Missouri legislature. Most of the people who had the tape were either police officers, or knew someone in law enforcement. Some said it happened in Denver, Arkansas or Lebanon, Mo. One source swore it was a Missouri Highway Patrol trooper.

They were all wrong.

The incident happened in the town of Poughkeepsie, N.Y., in February, 1974.

Lt. Lewis Deppner told me the story. "The legendary Al Clouser, now retired, was the officer on the tape. He was working the midnight tour.

"A man called and said a dog was chasing a deer. The deer ran in front of his car and he hit it. The man saw a hundred pounds of free meat. He threw the deer in the back seat. The deer came to life. He tried to stab it and hit it with a tire iron. The deer bit him. The dog chased him. He got into a phone booth and called the police."

The man grew hysterical as the conversation continued. When he talked about his wrecked car, he's almost crying.

The tape is hard to understand. Here's how the Poughkeepsie police translate it. One warning: It's loaded with four- and twelve-letter words. That MF is not a disease.

The Deer Hunter

MAN: Yeah, I need a man with a gun over here.
POLICE: You do?
MAN: I do. This MF. . . Let me explain what happened. This MF dog chased this deer, understand? And this MF chased this deer into my car. And I picked the deer up and put him in the back seat. And I was gonna take him and get him fixed, you understand? And that MF's tearing my gawd-damned car apart here.
P: Well, where's all this taking place?
M: You know where the Ford garage is? Route 9D? The Ford garage, where they sell them Fords? I got me a MF Cadillac out here, and this MF's tearing the shit out of the back seat. The MF bit me in the neck and that was it. I thought I was dead.
P: Well, where are you at?
M: I'm in a damn telephone booth. The MF dog chased me in a telephone booth, uh, he wants the damn deer. Damn!
P: Well, where are you at?
M: In the telephone booth, gawd damn it. I told you. Shit!
P: Where abouts?
M: I told you, at the Fords, where they sell them Fords over here. You know them cars? Fords.
P: Are you in the town of Poughkeepsie?
M: No! What?
P: Are you in the town of Poughkeepsie?
M: By the Mobil station. MoBEEL. I was in the gas station, the MF dog come back and chased me in the damn telephone booth.
P: OK, hang on a minute.
(Background noises, including a barking dog.)
P: Are you're sure it's not a Sunoco station?
M: Let me see. Yeah, that's what it is. A Sunoco station. This MF's done kicked my back window out. I just taked and put him in there to get him fixed, you understand?
P: Yeah. (laughing) You did that to take him home, I bet.
M: No, I just put him there to get him fixed and the dog come back and wanted him and he chased me in the MF telephone booth.
P: Well, hang in there. I'll send a car over.

M: This MF bit me, too. Send somebody with a gun to shoot him.
P: OK.
M: I stabbed him with my knife and hit him with a tire iron and he bit me good.
P: OK, we'll send a car over.
M: It's a big red Cadillac. You can't miss it 'cause the back window's knocked out.
P: OK.
M: That MF's thrashing and ripping my MF seat.

As the tape ends, you hear the police officer say, "You won't believe this . . ." That's how Lt. Deppner felt when he heard the official police tape the next morning.

"I made the first copy," he said. "We've been making tapes ever since. There must be 50,000 tapes out there. Scotland Yard has a tape. The White House has one. It's been in Canada and the FBI academy. I could imagine Eddie Murphy or Richard Pryor doing it as a comedy routine, but the funniest thing is, it's true."

One last question. What happened when the police arrived?

"By the time we got there, the guy was gone," Lt. Deppner said. "All we found was some auto glass, some seat stuffing, a little fur and a little blood. We've always wondered what he told his insurance company."

34. On the Couch

It isn't the bed that will determine the course of your marriage. It's the living-room couch.

Are you going to buy something that you can put your feet on?

Or will you get a museum piece in a light-colored fabric that looks good—as long as you don't sit on it?

The decorator couch often touches off domestic war. But a comfortable couch can produce a shabby sort of peace. The couch and your spouse start sagging about the same time. Before you know it, your living-room decor has begun the long slide from early American to late Archie Bunker.

Some women try to cover up the issue with slipcovers. These are an uncomfortable compromise.

There's really no way to do it right. But sometimes, you can go spectacularly wrong. Here is the truly hairy story of a South Side bride's first couch. She didn't tell me. Her sister snitched on her. She swears this story is true.

"My sister is still a newlywed," she said. "Her apartment is furnished with all the family odds and ends. But she saw an ad in the paper for a used living-room set. It had three upholstered pieces—a couch, a chair and a hassock—for $200. It was a wonderful bargain."

Maybe too wonderful.

"Yeah. I thought it sounded too good to be true. But newlyweds are kind of dumb. My sister and her husband went to look at the couch after work. She said it was perfect, a really neat nubby fabric. The colors were a great tweedy mix of beige, black and brown. That made it very practical. My brother-in-law is the outdoor type. He always forgets to take off his boots in the house.

"My sister doesn't want to spend her life nagging him. So she was looking for a couch that wouldn't show the dirt. Something he could lounge on and watch TV.

"Not only is this couch practical, it's pretty. My sister really liked the way it looked in the guy's living room. It was real atmospheric. He had two lights on, nice and romantic. The three or four cats sitting around made the place look lived in.

"They bought the set and found a friend with a truck to haul it home. Then they set it up in their living room. My sister turned on the ceiling light. She saw the sofa was awfully dirty. So she started vacuuming."

She was about to have a sweeping surprise. "The new sofa wasn't nubby. It wasn't tweedy and it wasn't a neat mixture of beige, black and brown. She's not sure what color it was. The lights were low in that 'atmospheric' living room so she couldn't see that the guy let his four cats sit on the sofa. It was covered with years of cat hair—more than she'd ever seen in her whole life.

"My sister hired a cleaning service to work on her couch. You've heard of them. They charge a flat fee of about $50 to clean your upholstery with a heavy-duty vacuum. It usually takes about fifteen minutes.

"The guy came in and started working on the living-room set. It went from nubby tweed to mangy beige. Big patches of beige upholstery were showing through the cover of cat hair.

"The guy worked for over an hour. By then the sofa was beige with polka-dots of cat hair.

"Finally he said, 'I've got to go, ma'am. My boss will kill me. I've already spent too much time here.'

"My sister looked at her polka-dot sofa and asked, 'What am I going to do?'

"The guy saw the scruffy living-room set and felt sorry for her. So he told her the facts of life about masking tape. He said you wind it around your hand, sticky side out, and start patting the upholstery. Masking tape will pick up the cat hair."

The young couple spent the night patting the furniture. It took them two or three evenings and several rolls of tape.

"At last she had this beautiful beige sofa with a chair and a matching ottoman. My sister says it's a real bargain, even if she did have to pay an extra $50 to have it vacuumed. Newlyweds can't expect furniture that good.

"It's a shame her husband can't sit on it, but you know how beige shows the dirt."

35. *Rover Looks So Natural*

I was looking for a greeting card at the shop. The cards were divided into the usual categories: Birthday, Anniversary, Sympathy, Death of a Pet.

Death of a what?

Pet. As in Spot, Rover, and Fluffy. When your friend's furry friend turns in its dinner dish, you can spend $1.15 for a Hallmark card expressing your sympathy.

The pet card was tastefully decorated with trees and birds, a motif suitable for either cats or dogs. It said:

"When a pet dies, that special warm place in our hearts suddenly becomes empty. . .

"And as in all painful events, it will take time to get over the loss . . .

"But there is something to hang on to. We realize that as time passes, animals have a way of teaching us about loving, about loyalty, joy and friendship. . .

"And whatever we've shared in their presence can never really be lost."

I couldn't agree more. That's why I hope Hallmark's Death of a Pet cards die quickly. Nothing against Hallmark. I know they mean well.

But we buy cards because they say what we should say. Greeting card sentiments usually don't have much to do with the truth. The nice thing about pets is you can always say your true feelings about them. And people still believe you.

When your dog dies, and you feel bad about it, you say, "Poor old Rover. Sorry he's gone. He was a good old dog."

Understanding friends will pat on you on the back and buy you a drink. You can toast Rover and feel better.

Or you can say, "My basset hound Charlie died. The kids loved him, but they never cleaned up after him. I did. Charlie spent most of his time eating me out of house and home."

You couldn't say that about one of your loved ones, even if it was true.

Unfortunately, we spend most of our time hiding our true feelings about humans. If someone reads in the paper that your Uncle Charlie died, and expresses sympathy, you can't say, "Tough luck about Charlie, but now that he's dead I get the Buick and 2,500 bucks."

It sounds crass.

Nor can you say, "Uncle Charlie? Don't waste your tears. One of the premier warts has been taken off the face of America."

If your dog Charlie suddenly turns vicious and begins tearing up the neighborhood, you can have him—what's the nice phrase?—"put to sleep." The neighbors will applaud you. Even call you civic-minded.

If you try that when Uncle Charlie gets nasty, some ingrate will call the cops.

That's the other nice thing about pets. They are convenient. Some people are revolted when otherwise sensible adults treat their pets like children. I admit I was startled when I heard some people talking about their kids, and one said, "My kid ran out of the house and hid under the car."

It turned out the kid in question was an orange cat.

Don H. was upset when a friend started telling his German shepherd, "Say hello to Uncle Don."

But then Don H. stared into the dog's big, trusting brown eyes and decided it didn't look any dumber than some of his real relatives.

Some say pets are like little people, only better: You don't have to buy them braces. You don't have send them to college. You don't have to answer their embarrassing questions.

Actually, pets are the way we wish kids were. Consider the common commands for dogs: Sit. Lie down. Fetch.

Those are all the things you can't get your own kids to do.

And when your dog reaches sixteen, and spends all day sitting around the house and drooling, it's OK to put him out in the yard, where you don't have to look at him.

One more thing worries me about pet cards. They could be the beginning of a pet death industry. The next thing you know we'll be at pet funeral homes, looking at the neighbor's Doberman and saying dumb things like, "He looks so natural." And, "It was for the best."

And that shouldn't happen to a dog.

36. Cat on a Software Roof

I've done so many animal stories, I should communicate in barks and growls. But I can't resist telling you about the Cat Food Flingers.

It started with two Clayton executives, Barbara Johnson and Jane McDonnell.

"I work in Clayton," Jane said. "From my office I can see the old Woolworth building. It was empty for awhile. One day, I saw a cat on the roof. I called an animal protection agency. They said they couldn't do much. No one occupied the building, so they couldn't set a trap and catch it.

"Jane and I started feeding the cat. Every night after work we'd leave a dish of food in the parking lot by the building. Somehow, the cat found its way down and ate it. But that roof was its home.

"The little guy seemed happy up there. It watched the people go by. We fed that animal in sleet, snow and rain. If we went on vacation someone fed it for us."

This went on for almost two years. "Then Egghead Discount Software moved into the building and a new cat showed up. Our cat wouldn't come down for its food any more. So we started throwing food on the roof. We'd wrap it loosely in plastic. Then we'd fling it.

"Every night at five, the cat would lean over the edge, meow and purr, and we'd fling the food.

"One night, we went over as usual to fling the food. A young man came out of Egghead Software. He said, 'I hope you're not feeding that cat.'

"We asked what was wrong with that. He said they were setting traps for it in the basement. We said if the cat was caught it would be destroyed. That didn't seem to bother him.

"He said if we continued to feed the cat he'd have to enforce the trespassing laws. I was all for calling the Clayton police right there. I wanted to see what the police would say about letting a cat starve on the roof. But Barbara didn't want a confrontation on the sidewalk.

"That cat deserves a chance. I'd hate to see it captured and put to sleep after two years on the roof. It's such a scraggy-looking animal. No one's going to adopt it. I can't take it because I have an old dog. And Barbara already has two cats."

Is Egghead Discount Software hardhearted?

"I'm not allowed to talk to reporters," the manager said, talking to a reporter. "It's against company policy."

I don't think Egghead has a policy on stray cats. So here's what he said.

"The cats are a nuisance. They get into our ceiling. They fall asleep on the ceiling tiles and when we flip on the store lights they get scared and jump up. One almost fell through. I can't have cats dropping through the ceiling and hitting people on the head."

It could cause bad felines.

"I don't want to feed them," he said. "It's not my responsibility to keep them alive. The Humane Society said they could have rabies. From a business standpoint, you can't have diseased cats falling out of the ceiling. I could get sued.

"One large cat has already been caught. That's the one that almost fell through. Another one lives on the roof. All it does is hiss at me.

"Those two ladies were very belligerent. They wouldn't move. If they were insulted, I apologize."

Jane and Barbara don't want an apology. "We want the cat to have a chance. In all fairness, I realize Egghead had to do something. But that cat survived two years on the roof. You just can't let it die."

Well, some people could. But Dr. Dan Knox at St. Louis County Animal Control isn't one of them. He had a humane solution. He said he would have the cat trapped. Then, if it wasn't too wild, he would try to find it a home. If it was sick, he'd have to destroy it.

Jane and Barbara said that was fair. The store manager agreed. I didn't ask the cat.

The next day, the cat was captured. Four days later, Dr. Knox delivered his opinion. He said the cat seems to be a fairly healthy female. "It's not a friendly, cuddly cat. It's not a cat for children. It's fairly aggressive.

"I would be willing to work with someone who has had experience with animals—provided they didn't hold us responsible for any problems. I'd have to evaluate the situation first. The cat is probably best on a farm or a remote area."

What a deal—a free ugly, aggressive cat. All you had to do is throw it a little food.

Five people volunteered to take the cat. It went to a woman in West County who had ten dog-free acres. She named it Slinger. The two executives who kept it alive by flinging cat food on the roof have visiting privileges.

The cat seems content in its new home. After all, it's already had its fling in the city.

37. Squatter Moles

The two brothers, one city, one suburban, were sitting around with some barbecue and a few brews. The suburban brother began talking about a problem that pops up every spring.

Dandelions?

"Worse," said the city brother. "Moles. They ruin his lawn every year. He asked me if I had the same problem. I said, 'No, I live in the city. Our yards are only thirty-five feet wide. The moles just whip on through, and head on down the road. Then they're somebody else's problem.'

"But suburban Chesterfield is different. It's got those big yards. My brother has two acres. His lawn is so big the moles get confused and start running around in circles."

Every year, he tries to beat the moles. Every year he fails. He comes up with clever ideas to shock, choke, poison, drive them away and drive them crazy. It sounds a little like that movie *Caddyshack*. Except the Chesterfield moles make the golf course gopher look like a pussy cat.

"This is the last spring my brother's going to try," he said. "He's going to give it one more year, and then he's going to give it up. You can't believe what he's spent on it. He says if mole meat were in style, it would cost him $1,000 a pound."

I don't know if that price includes car repairs. The car was damaged in last year's anti-mole campaign.

"That's the year he was going to gas them. His wife has this little Ford Fiesta. My brother hitched up a garden hose to the car exhaust and shoved it down the burrow. The back pressure blew out the car's manifold. It cost $150 to fix."

Score one for the moles.

"But my brother still liked the gassing idea, even if it broke his wife's car. And he wasn't about to use his Corvette. But he had another brilliant idea: He'd use his outboard motor.

"An outboard motor doesn't work unless it's in water. So he put it in a fifty-five-gallon trash can, and ran the garden hose down the mole hole again. But when his kids switched it on, they didn't put the motor in neutral. It was in gear. The blades chopped up the trash can."

It didn't help the motor, either.

The score was Moles 2, Chesterfield, 0.

"Another year, he tried to drown the moles. My brother heard if you put a garden hose down the hole and turned on the water, they'd drown. His moles must wear scuba gear. He ran the water for three hours and nothing happened."

To the moles. The results to the lawn were dramatic. "It turned into a big, soggy trench."

Score 3 for the moles.

"Then he tried poison peanuts. You buy them pre-poisoned. They're blue. If you ever see a blue nut, that's no stale pistachio—it's poison. My brother put the poisoned peanuts on top the burrow, then pounded them down in with a hammer and a stake.

"The moles are supposed to eat the peanuts and die. But these moles were either very clean or very smart. They pushed all the peanuts back out again.

"The garden shop said it was my brother's fault. He touched the peanuts with his fingers, and the moles could smell him. They don't like people's food, just their grass."

It was now Moles 4, Chesterfield zip. His fifth attempt was a shocking failure. "He planted an electric device in the moles' burrow to shock them. The moles just scooted around it.

"Then this year he got the ultimate weapon."

I saw the movie. Nuclear weapons.

"Nope, it's an electronic device. You put it down the mole hole and it makes a weird noise to drive them away. Supposed to sound like a mole in distress or something.''

The latest in anti-mole technology cost him $49. ''But my brother says he can't lose. If it doesn't work, he'll sell it to our father for $39.''

How does it feel to be outwitted by something that weighs maybe five ounces?

''Oh, my brother's got a great way to work out his frustrations. He goes to the Showbiz Pizza Place and plays this kid's game called Wac-A-Demon. The 'demon' is a mole.

''The game is about the size of your desk, except it's full of holes. The mole comes out about three inches, and you try to whack it on the head with a rubber mallet. He finds it very soothing.''

38. The Day the Cat Rode the Pigeon

My mother-in-law, God rest her soul, believed some day Don H. and I would turn into a normal couple. So the day the cat rode a pigeon into the kitchen, all her hopes were blasted.

By ''normal'' she meant Don H. and I would give up our slightly raffish writers' life, settle down, and turn into a scene from ''Leave It to Beaver.'' June Cleaver would stand at the door of our city flat and wait for Ward in pearls and a sweater. (What Ward was doing in pearls and a sweater is beyond me.)

Once Ward was in the door, I would fix him a nice roast for dinner. My mother-in-law thought red meat was the key to sensible living.

It was too late for us to change, but there was no reason why she had to be unhappy. All it took was a phone call. She lived in Marshalltown, Iowa, and we lived in St. Louis. We used to give her a regular Sunday ''it's OK, Mom, we're normal'' call.

This was a two-part performance. First, Don H. would give her an edited version of the week's events.

Then I would describe a mythical Sunday dinner. I didn't cook, but I could read. I got a basic cookbook. When my mother-in-law would ask, ''What's for dinner this Sunday?'' I would open the cook book to the index and say, ''Pork, Roast.''

''And how are you going to fix it?'' she would ask, encouragingly. She always talked me through these meals.

''I plan to preheat the oven to 375, then score the roast with a sharp knife,'' I would begin, until I'd read her the entire recipe.

Never mind. It gave the poor woman peace of mind. It gave us peace and quiet. And it worked until that fateful summer Sunday.

While Don H. was going into Part One of the phone call, I was upstairs cleaning out the attic. This was such a normal activity, it was the first item on his weekly report.

Suddenly, I heard horrible screams coming from the kitchen. It was Don H., yelling at the top of his voice, "Elaine! Elaine! Quick. Come down here. The cat is riding a pigeon."

At least, that's what it sounded like. I came running down the steps just in time to hear Don H. tell his mother, "I've got to hang up, Mom. The cat is riding a pigeon. I'll explain later."

I had no idea how he was going to explain that one. A huge, fat, red-eyed city pigeon was waddling in from the dining room. It must have gotten in through an open attic window.

And sitting on its back was our small orange tiger cat, Hodge. Hodge weighed about a pound less than the pigeon. He was an indoor cat. The only bird call he knew was the sound of a can opener on a Banquet country chicken dinner. Some instinct told him to catch the bird. But it didn't say what to do next. So the cat sat on the pigeon like a circus bareback rider. No, he wasn't that graceful. Hodge was terrified and hung on like he was drowning.

The pigeon wasn't scared at all. It looked indignant. It waddled into the kitchen and stood there. It looked at me. The cat looked at me. So did Don H. They all expected me to do something.

I grabbed a broom, separated the cat from his catch, and scooted the pigeon out the back door. It sat on the porch for a moment, then flew off unharmed. The cat looked relieved.

Don H. looked worried. He had to call his mother back and explain what happened. She laughed. But she never sounded quite the same. She wasn't reassured by our "everything is normal, Mom" phone calls any more.

But at least she never figured out the Sunday dinners were in alphabetical order.

FOOD
& OTHER
WEIGHTY
ISSUES

39. The $3,114 Turkey Dinner

I've never been much good at saving money. But this year, I tried to quit spending. Cold turkey.

That's how I wound up with a $3,114 turkey dinner.

The savings spree started after the Christmas bills showed up. "We have to save some money," Don H. decreed. I knew just how to do it. We would eat in.

Don H., bless him, hates home cooking. Which is fortunate, because even if he liked it, he'd hate mine. Luckily we live on the South Side, a neighborhood with good, cheap restaurants.

But I knew a painless way to save. I would roast a turkey. The instructions are printed right on the side. And leftover turkey tastes great. We could get several dinners and lunches.

"Fine," said Don H. "I'll buy the turkey and you roast it."

That was my first mistake. No woman sends a hungry man alone to the supermarket. Don H. really gave me the bird. He came home with a turkey that weighed twenty-seven pounds, twelve ounces. Enough to feed an army barracks.

"Don't worry," Don H. said. "I'm hungry." He'd be even hungrier when he finally ate the turkey. It was still frozen. I read the defrosting instructions. If we used the "refrigerator method" the twenty-seven pound turkey would be thawed in six days. If we used the "cold water method" I could cook it in forty-eight hours. I left it out on the kitchen sink and hoped for a heat wave.

That night, we still ate at home—we ordered pizza. Day 1 of our money-saving plan had cost us forty-seven bucks, including the turkey and the pizza tip.

By Sunday afternoon, the turkey looked defrosted. It was so big it wouldn't fit in a roasting pan. So I put it on a cookie sheet.

"I still think it's frozen inside," said Don H.

I ignored him coldly. I knew what I was doing. I'd even remembered to remove the giblets. But I forgot about the neck at the other end. That's why, one hour into the roasting, the oven sprung a leak.

The ice in the neck cavity was melting. And the turkey neck was imbedded in the ice. I wrestled the turkey upright and chipped out the frozen

neck. It's not easy to get burned and frostbitten at the same time.

In a few hours, the turkey was nice and brown. What I could see of it. The house was filled with smoke. The basting juices overflowed the cookie sheet and ran down the oven onto the floor.

At eleven that night, the turkey was finally roasted. It looked beautiful. It tasted good, too. And this dinner didn't cost a dime. The entertainment was also free. We spent the evening mopping the floor.

The next night we planned to eat at home. But when we lit the oven more smoke billowed out. Obviously, it needed to be cleaned. This was a job for a pro. We ate dinner out, then called a cleaning service. It took two people one hour to clean the oven. But the price was a bargain—$30.

Dinner and the oven cleaning brought the price of the turkey up to $114.

The next night we stayed home and ate leftover turkey. For the first time in months, we got a good look at the kitchen. Don H. noticed the table was old and battered. "We really ought to buy a new one," he said.

Not until we get a new stove. Do you know how old it is?

"Maybe we could sell it as an antique," he said.

Once we move the stove we'll have to get new linoleum.

"Yeah, it doesn't look too good, either. But a new floor, a new stove and a new table could cost $3,000 easy."

We should start saving money for it, I said.

"There's another way to save," he said. "Let's forget the new kitchen and go out to dinner."

40. Bouncing off the Ceiling

You could say Walter Henkel is the toast of the town. And he owes it all to a visit from his mother.

"Aww," he said. "I didn't do anything. It's just that us Germans never throw anything away."

Walter's mother gave him an old toaster when he got out of the army in 1965.

"It worked fine for a year," Walter said. "Then it started toasting only the inner side of the bread. So I took it apart, found the broken wire and fixed it.

"I tested it without bread, and it seemed fine. Then I put it back together again and set it on the kitchen counter."

The key phrase here is "seemed fine." Walter didn't realize he'd damaged the toaster when he was tinkering. "It was an important part, too. When the toast pops up, this device keeps it from flying up and hitting the ceiling.

"The next morning, I was making breakfast and getting dressed for work. I put the toast in, and went out of the room. I heard the toaster go off. I came back in and there's no bread. I looked all over the kitchen and couldn't find it.

"So I put in two more pieces and watched it. The bread came flying out, bounced off the underside of the kitchen cabinets and fell in the crack between the sink and the wall. I got a flashlight, looked down, and there were the other two missing pieces of toast."

So you took the toaster apart and fixed it?

"No. That's too hard," Walter said. Only true handy persons talk this way. They spend hours fixing things for friends and customers. But they don't waste time on themselves.

"If I was fixing the toaster for someone else, I'd go through all that. But it belonged to me. So I moved the toaster out of the way of the cabinets and let the toast bounce off the ceiling. Then I'd catch it on the way down."

Walter's system was simple but effective. It also improved his hand-eye coordination. And since he lived alone, there was no problem teaching anyone else how the toaster worked.

For the next eight years Walter continued to catch some toast in the morning. "Then my mother came for a visit," Walter said. "She gets up early. I was in that state where you're half awake but aware of everything that's going on. I heard her moving around the kitchen. She put the coffee on. Then she put the bread in the toaster."

That's when Walter woke up completely.

"I forgot to warn her about the toaster. I was about to rush out to the kitchen when I heard the thing go off. First there was a THUMP! That's when it hit the ceiling. Then there was a WHUMP! WHUMP!

"The first whump was when it hit the toaster. The second when it bounced off and hit the radiator. Then it hit the floor. I heard my mother say. . . well, never mind what she said. But I thought I'd better not go in the kitchen for awhile."

About twenty minutes later, Walter finally got the courage to get out of bed.

"My mother said, 'What kind of toaster is that? It chased me all over the room.' My mother exaggerates."

Walter's mother popped for a new toaster. Walter put it away in the box. It stayed there for years.

"My old toaster was just fine," he said. "It finally wore out last year. Nothing worked any more. It wouldn't flip the toast up to the ceiling. It just sat there and burned."

Walter brought out the "new" toaster—now about 14 years old.

"The new one is just not as good," he said. "It doesn't toast the bread evenly. I still keep the old one on the kitchen counter. I can't bear to throw it away. Some day I may restore it to its former glory."

41. How to Lose Weight Without Dieting

Admit it. You've never had a runner's high. There may be a rush from your aerobics class, but it's for the door.

But one thing does make you feel good: losing weight. When you flop your flab onto the scale and find there's a low-fat content, it's a real high.

But you're getting this good news less and less these days. Scales don't seem to be accurate any more. The darn things say you've put on weight. That can't be right. You've been on a strict diet. Except for that pound of Oreo cookies, and you ate them with your fingers crossed.

I used to have the same problem, until I realized scales are delicate instruments. To get the reading you want, you need to adjust them. I guarantee if you use my weigh-in tips, you'll lose at least ten pounds overnight. They're a dramatic solution to a weighty problem.

Ten Ways to Give Yourself a Fat Chance

1. Take it off. Take it all off. Those gym socks and underwear add unnecessary pounds. If you must keep that towel modestly around your middle, remember terry is very absorbent. Your towel has soaked up a lot of bath water. Subtract five pounds.

2. You're still loaded with excess weight. Gold is a heavy element. Take off that watch, necklace and wedding ring. Some people remove the wedding ring permanently and get rid of more than a hundred pounds of ugly fat.

3. Take off your glasses, unless you need them to read the scale. In that case, weight watching is a heavy duty. Subtract another pound.

4. You can't remove the fillings in your teeth. Remember how the dentist pounded them in? Subtract those pounds.

5. Hit the bathroom before you hit the scale. Flush out some hidden weight.

6. I bet you're holding your breath when you step onto that scale. Exhale. Air isn't all that light.

7. Cut your hair. You'd be surprised what a weight you have on your mind. A trim will shave off several ounces. If you have very long hair, cut it short and you'll be at least a pound lighter.

8. Give blood. The American Red Cross says you lose 1.2 pounds every time you give blood. They also said the loss is temporary, but I hung up before the spokesperson could give the depressing explanation.

9. Make children part of the fitness process early. Teach your child to lie on the floor and push up on one corner of the scale. This exercise improves the kid's hand-eye coordination and corrects the unfortunate slope in the bathroom floor that throws off your scale and makes you fat.

This exercise works best with very young children. The older ones talk.

10. Tell yourself muscle weighs more than fat. I've discovered I build the most muscle after carbo-loading foods made with natural ingredients, such as pizza and beer.

Must be all those 12-ounce curls.

42. *You Can't Get Married Without It*

Many people treat my neighborhood, the South Side, like a foreign country.

No wonder. We South Siders speak our own language (youse guys, sunda and warsh). We have our own colorful customs, especially at weddings and funerals. I haven't died yet, but I did have a typical South Side wedding.

The reception was held in a VFW hall. The guest list included 400 wedding and funeral relatives. About half of them weren't speaking to the other half. There was one outrageous middle-aged woman in hot pants. And one drunken uncle. The family posted guards on the uncle, to make sure he didn't say anything awful.

These are entertaining, but the real delight of the South Side wedding is a massive buffet. Leave your diet at home. It's time to feast on ham, roast beef, dollar rolls, two kinds of potato salad, cole slaw, and mostaccioli, pronounced MUSK-a-choli. Mostaccioli tastes like spaghetti, with fatter noodles.

If you want to get snitzy, you add some form of fried chicken, usually wings or drumsticks.

A reader I'll call Harry is worried that our native customs may be disappearing.

"I'm not from the South Side," Harry said, "but I was invited to a South Side wedding, and I knew what to expect. At first, I thought it had everything, even the obligatory unmarried woman wearing a knit dress, who shouldn't have.

"Until we got to the buffet. It had no ham and no fried chicken, and worst of all, no mostaccioli. Apparently in an attempt to appeal to the yuppie, they'd substituted pasta con broccoli.

"I was all set to swine out. Instead I got sliced turkey and pasta. It was bland," Harry said. "I'm afraid this is a trend, and young South Siders are rejecting the old ways and turning yuppie. I'm also worried the couple may not be legally married without mostaccioli."

Well, this is serious. I consulted my South Side social expert, Janet Smith. First, I asked her if the couple was legally married without mostaccioli.

"If the grandma or the aunt with all the jewelry was there, the mar-

riage was legal," Janet said. "She would make sure the couple had a real minister, and if necessary, administer the mostaccioli later.

"Remember the trend in the sixties and seventies for the couple to recite their own vows? The aunts and grandmas made sure those weddings were legal, too. And they had the satisfaction of outliving that trend."

Are mostaccioli-less weddings a South Side trend?

"No. It was probably done by someone who was not raised on the South Side. Some neighborhoods have new money. We have new South Siders. They try to be like us, but there's always something a little bit off. It's possible they went to the wrong caterer. Or perhaps they got a better deal with the pasta con broccoli. Saving money is very South Side.

"But I assure you, this is not a trend," Janet said. "When my daughter gets married, I'll have the traditional buffet, complete with mostaccioli."

Great. When's the wedding?

"I don't know. She's 11 years old."

43. Dinner for a Dollar

Every week Jack Grone dines in the city's show places. He likes the richest delicacies: Jumbo shrimp. Roast beef. Cheddar cheese and fresh fruit.

Jack is twenty-two and just starting his career. Right now, his wallet is as flat as his stomach, and food like this can eat into a young man's budget. But not Jack's.

"I eat dinner for a dollar," he said. "I'm in the best places in town, and I pay almost nothing."

It won't cost him anything to share his secret. "I eat at Happy Hour after work. One night, I went to Menage, the dance club at Union Station. I ordered a club soda with lime. It cost me a buck. And I can go to the free buffet.

"This was on a Monday. The place was deserted, and there's 200 pounds of food out. I went back five times. I finally stopped because people were staring at me."

Aren't you embarrassed?

"Not at all," Jack said. "It's perfectly legal. And if the restaurant gets mad, I move on to some other place. I hit a different one each night. There are dozens of them.

"If you're feeling classy, you splurge and get a mixed drink. You can eat your way across town for $2.50. The waiters will serve you a drink and then bother you a few times until they figure out what you're doing. Then they stand in the back and laugh at you.

"I don't care. They're probably doing the same thing on their day off."

There is one moment when Jack feels a slight flicker of shame. "The worst is when the waiter brings your check for $2.50, and you whip out a credit card. Waiters get a little ticked at the paperwork. Every month you get a Visa bill three pages long, and it's all $2.50 charges."

Jack sees hunting Happy Hour as a transitional phase. "My friends are either still in college or just starting work. Nobody has any money.

"In college, 'drinking' means hanging out at the frat house and downing 20 beers until you barf. At a Happy Hour, you 'have a drink.' It's more sophisticated.

"I go for the cheap eats. After a day at the office, I'm tired. My microwave is on strike. I don't feel like cooking. I can have dinner for a dollar, and somebody else does the dishes.

"The name Happy Hour is ridiculous. It's more like Oh Happy Day. The hour gets longer and longer. Maggie O'Brien's has two happy hours. One is 4 to 6:30 P.M., the other 12:30 to 2 A.M. Pretty soon it's going to be 9 to 5."

Jack has a regular circuit. "A group of us go to one place for shrimp on Thursdays. At another good place you pay a dollar and get pizza, potato skins and nachos."

You do get around.

"Seriously, I don't know how these places make any money off people like me."

Most St. Louis places say they don't mind the freeloaders. "We get the people in here, and that's all that counts," said Maggie O'Brien's.

In some cities, saloons have wised up. Some Washington D.C. bars charge about $5 for a "Hungry Hour."

A manager at the Fedora Cafe and Bar said he tolerates the "dollar diners." "At least this gentleman had the courtesy to buy a club soda. Some don't even do that," he said. "It really upsets the waiters. It cuts into their tips. And it makes it difficult for the people who do buy drinks. A year ago, we didn't charge a dollar for our buffet. Now it helps with the cost.

"But I do believe what goes around comes around. Someday, this young man may be doing well enough to buy a whole dinner. And then I hope he remembers Fedora's has those, too."

44. Eight Signs of a Second-Rate Restaurant

Don H. and I were sitting down to dinner at a fine restaurant. At least, everyone said it was fine. It had stars and diamonds and rave reviews.

But Don H. noticed something was wrong. It wasn't a swinging place. The swinging door between the kitchen and the dining room was wedged open.

"The food is going to be awful," he said, mysteriously. "They've propped open the kitchen door."

That's ridiculous, I said. The chef is highly rated.

"When a restaurant props open the kitchen door," Don H. said, "they don't care any more. It's one sign the place is sliding."

He was right. Through those non-swinging doors came the finest Alpo money could buy. It was covered with a trendy raspberry sauce, but it was still dog food. The place closed three months later.

But that awful dinner wasn't wasted. I learned one way to tell a second-rate restaurant.

Nowadays, when you need a loan to take the family out to dinner, you can't afford a bad meal. Reviews and recommendations aren't enough. You need my **Eight Sure Signs of a Second-Rate Restaurant.** They work whether you're eating in a cafe or a candlelight restaurant.

1. Watch out for any place that calls itself "down-home" or "country."

That's usually an excuse for cheap food and sloppy service. You can trust almost any restaurant that calls itself a cafe, if it's more than twenty years old. EAT is another good sign.

2. The French Connection.

Unless the owner's name is Claude or Pierre, *soup du jour* should be the only French phrase on the menu. Fractured French isn't sophisticated. It usually translates as mediocre food with outrageous prices.

Restaurants that call French fries *pommes frites* are always pretentious.

3. A big menu doesn't mean the chef is creative.

It means an eighteen-year-old kid is shoving food into a microwave. Chinese restaurants are the only exception.

4. Beware of places that put the staff in funny costumes.

Unless you're hiking in the Black Forest, you shouldn't see young men in lederhosen. Underneath that gemutlich costume is an embarrassed kid from the suburbs. Ditto for the waitress in the dirndl.

It's cruel to make the staff dress like hillbillies, cowboys or English serving wenches. Even worse, the restaurant is probably making the staff pay for their humiliation. They may have to buy those silly outfits.

5. Music duels.

Two kinds of music are another sour note. When you hear sweet strings on the restaurant's piped-in music, and hard rock coming from the radio in the kitchen, nobody's in charge.

6. Disaster relief.

Any restaurant can have an occasional disaster. A roach may stroll across your table. The kitchen may lose your order. It happens.

But the good restaurants buy you a drink or a free dessert. Any place

that hands you only an apology isn't sorry—it's downright pathetic.

7. Managers are not ornamental.

At good restaurants, the managers help out during a rush. They'll get a check, pour coffee or clear a table.

When you see overworked waiters rushing around while the manager stands there doing nothing, watch out. The manager is too good to work. This place is run just like your office. Would you want to eat there?

8. Food for thought.

When you sit down to your $40 plate of pasta, you may feel the staff is laughing at you. There's no reason to feel uneasy. I have dined in restaurants from Shanghai to San Francisco and I can reassure you—they are laughing at you.

But the good ones never let you know it.

45. Daddy, What's Curb Service?

Something shocking happened in Laurie's office. "One of the guys came in and told us about his fourteen-year-old daughter, Sheila. It was horrible.

"Sheila was going through a box of his things when she found a big white card with black numbers.

"She said, 'What's that, Dad?'

"He said, 'That's from Steak 'n Shake. They put it on your windshield for curb service.'

"She said, 'What's curb service, Dad?' "

What's curb service? She didn't know. And Dad didn't know any place where he could show her. He took the awful news to the office. It couldn't be true. They began calling their favorite places. White Castle discontinued curb service years ago. So did Parkmoor. Carl's Drive Inn stopped fifteen years ago. None of their neighborhood Steak 'n Shakes had curb service any more.

"We're not even forty yet, and we've outlived something," Laurie said. "Please find it again."

Curb service was more than a way to eat. It was a way of life. A teenage ritual.

In North County, where I grew up, the best place to encounter curb service was at the Steak 'n Shake on North Lindbergh.

It took a lot of courage to go there. Only cool kids circled Steak. What if the secret nerd detector at the entrance caught you?

Today, kids meet in the mall. But circling Steak required real strategy. First, you picked up three or four of your girlfriends and stopped at McDonald's for hamburgers. McD's burgers were cheaper than Steak's, but you didn't want anyone to see you there.

Then you headed down the highway, and made the circle through Steak's parking lot. One trip through, and you knew who was going steady, who was breaking up and who was stepping out.

Where you parked was important. Only geeks and parents parked close to the building. The best spots were around the edges.

When the carhop showed up, you checked out the males to see if they were cute. You examined the females for beauty secrets. Where did she find that wonderful corpse-green eye shadow? And your mother would never let you walk around in pants that tight.

That's probably why you were with your girlfriends on Saturday night.

Then you placed your order: One Coke, three glasses of water, two orders of fries. The whole thing came to under $2 for four people.

The carhop put a numbered card on your windshield, brought your order on a metal tray and hooked it to the window. You had to roll it down, just so.

Then you sat back and watched the show. The hottest cars in the neighborhood would come screeching through, mufflers roaring. Tangerine Mustangs. GTOs. Evil black Corvettes. You'd heard about a kid whose dad not only bought him a Vette for his birthday—he paid the insurance, too.

Maybe there would be a miracle. A guy (gasp) might come over to your car (giggle) and say hello.

When you got ready to leave, you piled up your wrappers and napkins real high, so the carhop wouldn't notice you were stealing the Steak glass.

No wonder curb service died. Almost.

It survives in a few spots. The best place to see it is probably Chuck-A-Burger in North County. It's had curb service since 1957. It still does, from 10 A.M. to 10 P.M. daily.

Steak 'n Shake said the drive-in window killed their curb service. But their customers missed it so much, a few Steaks tried to bring it back.

One of the most successful revivals is the Chesterfield Steak. They have curb service every day at lunch, but it may stop when the weather turns cold.

So Sheila's dad can show his daughter curb service.

But do you want to? Remember when your parents tried to be pals and took you to Steak? You knew it was social death if your friends saw you.

Don't do it, Dad. It's no fun eating hamburgers on the car floor.

46. Poison at Dinner

We were having dinner in a restaurant when a woman sat down at the table next to us. Her perfume rolled across the room in great clouds, like chemical warfare.

Ugh, I said, choking. That's Poison.

"It is pretty strong," said my dinner partner mildly. "But I don't think it will kill you."

You don't understand. That woman is wearing the perfume, Poison, the deadliest perfume since White Shoulders. It can kill taste buds at fifty paces. It is worn mostly by the nasally impaired. They have no idea they are choking other diners.

Would you light up a cigarette? I asked my dinner partner.

"I thought you didn't smoke," she said.

I don't. But I hate perfume more. I'll take cancer over Poison any day.

She set to work, creating a smoke screen between me and Grim Reeker.

Many restaurants now have smoking and non-smoking sections. It's a start. But there's room for other improvements. I'd also like to propose perfume and non-perfume sections.

This section would not discriminate against women. Men aren't any better. Some of them slather on the aftershave and cologne. And while I'm on my (nonperfumed) soapbox, there's one other smelly object I'd like removed from restaurants.

Children.

I know your own children are exceptionally well-behaved. It's other people's kids. It's awful sitting next to a table with all that shrieking, screaming, and slobbering.

And those are just the parents. The kids are even worse.

Consider the unhappy parents who save up for a night away from the children. They hire a babysitter, who charges slightly less than a kidnapper. They get dressed up. They go to a romantic restaurant. And they wind up next to a table full of squalling kids.

I realize there is a time and a place for children. I'd recommend the White Castle parking lot at 3 A.M.

I'm not talking about fast-food restaurants, pizza joints, and any place that calls itself a "family restaurant." Those are fair game. I mean nice restaurants, with tablecloths and waiters. In those places, the unofficial children's hour is over around 7 o'clock. After that, the kids are supposed to clear out and let the grownups eat by themselves.

That's my plan for restaurant improvement. I think it should be started immediately. I know some will say no-smoking, no-perfume, no-children sections will make restaurant seating too complicated.

That's not true.

The only real problem would be with perfumed, cigar-smoking kids.

THE
BURBS

47. The Closet Lover

Psychologist Dean L. Rosen was discussing his feelings. "I have this sense of selling out," he said. "I feel ashamed. My friends don't even want to talk about it."

What did you do, Dean? "I moved to the suburbs."

There's no reason for it, I know. But people who live in the city feel culturally superior to those in the suburbs. Dean was proud of his elegant city apartment. Now he lives in a subdivision.

Why did you do it, Dean? Were you worried about city crime? Or poor schools?

"No," he said. "I did it for the closets."

Closets?

"My subdivision house has big eight-foot closets. And a dressing room."

I whimpered. That's cruel, Dean. My city house has three tiny closets.

But he showed no mercy. He began describing his suburban house in intimate detail.

"I traded character and charm for convenience. My subdivision house has a double-car garage with an automatic opener."

Stop it.

"And the garage is attached. I can go right into the kitchen in the winter without getting cold and wet.

"In the summer I have central air conditioning, instead of little window units that you have to take in and out. This summer I took my vacation at Sears and bought a twenty-cubic-foot refrigerator with an ice maker. Now I have every appliance but one. I still won't buy a trash compactor. And we get by with one VCR."

That's rough, Dean.

"What's rougher is no one envies me. All my city friends act as if I've done something embarrassing. Our parents were glad to leave the dirty old city. But baby boomers feel guilty, like we're abandoning it."

Dean says life in the suburbs is very different.

"In the city, people use their feet as transportation. A walk has a destination. You go for a walk to buy an ice cream cone, a beer, or a pack of cigarettes. That doesn't happen in the suburbs. For one thing, there is no place to walk to. There are no stores within walking distance of most large subdivisions. In some places, there aren't even sidewalks. However, everyone is out walking at all hours of the day and night. These suburbanites are serious, hard-core walkers. They walk for health and fitness.''

That's something else Dean noticed. Suburban people look different.

"In the city, people wear their self-indulgence proudly. Beer guts aren't hidden behind oversized sports togs. The suburbs also have overweight people, but they can't enjoy it and would never flaunt it. Designer labels, yes. Fat, no.

"Since subdivision kids can't walk to a store for a soda or Popsicle, their parents stock their freezers with these treats. But they rob their children of the wonderful experience of picking and choosing and buying. Subdivision kids also have less opportunity to steal from the corner store. They don't experience all the pain and guilt for succumbing to temptation.''

You'd think most people would be happy to skip that, but Dean the psychologist says kids may "even be developmentally arrested if they are not given an opportunity to face this crisis of childhood.''

Dean says city kids take public buses. "Suburban kids have to depend on their parents to take them everywhere. Maybe that's why more young adults are living at home depending on their parents instead of moving out on their own.

"Life appears to be too clear-cut in the suburbs. You grow up and marry and have kids. Real life has so many more alternatives.

"When I first moved out here, I used to find it odd to be surrounded by nothing but white people. But I'm getting used to it.''

He's also getting used to all the Republicans.

Strangest of all, he's happy in his suburban home. There's just one more thing that Dean needs to make his life complete.

"I want to win the Yard of the Month. The winner gets a sign on the lawn for all your friends to snicker at or envy.

"I covet it. I've never won it yet, and I want to. I even got a lawn service. The grass really is greener on my side.''

48. Talking Your Way Out of Tickets

I've finally learned to play a pretty good game of poker. Now I want to learn how to talk my way out of traffic tickets.

I've asked people who are good at it for tips. "Be polite,'' they tell me. "Cops are basically nice folks.''

I try to stay calm. But my palms get sweaty. I drop stuff. I look guilty. I get a ticket.

The people who talk their way out of tickets don't say anything special—they are special. Rich kids. When they were growing up, their daddies could afford lawyers. Their families could make trouble. Of course, they'd never say this to a police officer. They don't have to. It's an attitude.

As soon as I'm stopped by a cop, I turn into what I really am. A sweaty suburban kid. With no lawyers. And no rich, indulgent parents.

Suburban teenagers were the natural targets of bad cops. Especially in the sixties. They amused themselves by stopping teenagers. They'd find some minor offense: broken taillight, noisy muffler, failure to use a turn signal. If you looked real scared, the cop would let you go with a ticket. If you talked smart, they might search your car for that ounce of oregano.

Chuck McHenry is another one of us. He's a fairly substantial citizen now—he's a dentist. "But I used to be a hippie. That's why I always look guilty when the police stop me.

"I've tried everything," he said. "The psychologists say you should get out of your car as soon as you stop and walk over to the officer's car. This puts the officer in the seated (or power) position, and makes you the supplicator in the inferior (or pleading) position. Sort of like a king in court."

In the sixties, Chuck could make the copper feel like the king of the road.

"Then they started shooting troopers on the highway," he said. "And I noticed as I opened my door in my rush to get to the throne the officers were dropping behind their car doors and reaching for their pistols."

The king was dead.

"In the seventies, I used a variation on the standard 'Take out your wallet' routine. I'd flip it open a la Star Trek and say, 'Beam me up, Scotty.' That brought a smile and a more lenient attitude."

Are cops secret Trekkies?

"No. It just sounded cute. And it worked for a while. Until the eighties. That's when you had to wear seat belts or get another ticket. I couldn't be cute any more, because I was fumbling to put my seat belt on. I had to sneak it under my left armpit and hope the officer didn't notice.

"Once I tried being indignant. The trooper said I was going fifty-seven in a fifty-five mile-an-hour zone. I knew I wasn't speeding. So I demanded, 'What's your badge number? What troop are you with?' and he backed off.

"Then I tried it again when I really was speeding, and I was nailed. It was a total disaster. It still hurts just to think about it.

"My wife Linda K. is a feminist in most respects. But she cries when she's caught, and it works almost every time. I thought about crying.

You know, being sensitive. But like all men who get pulled over, I immediately assume I'm guilty. That feeling overwhelms me so much the tears just won't come."

Even the truth is no defense. "Once in New Mexico, I was driving my old '73 Dodge van and I got pulled over for speeding. That was impossible. My old van couldn't go over fifty-five. He was just pulling me over because I had out-of-state plates.

" 'But officer,' I said, 'this car won't do fifty-five with the pedal to the metal.'

" 'Then you can tell it to the judge,' he said.

" 'When can I do that?' I said.

" 'Wednesday a week from now,' he said.

"I couldn't wait around that long. I left. I thought I would be out of state, out of mind. Until they sent me a second warrant for my arrest. Then I paid. You never can tell when you may want to go to New Mexico again."

Chuck has had one success. "I live in a rural area, so I tried a good old boy approach when I got stopped by a cop with an Ozark drawl. I asked where he was from. I knew somebody from his town. We got to talking and the next thing you know, he wasn't giving me a ticket.

"But now that I'm a solid citizen, I'm starting to look like a yuppie, so my good old boy routine doesn't work, either. You can't win."

49. When the Suits Take Over

Four days a week, Judy is a downtown executive. But one day—Monday—she's a suburban mom with two little girls, ages two and four.

"I like to do my marketing on Monday, so I don't have to drag the kids to the store on the weekend," Judy said.

I appreciate it. We all do. Judy understands how most people really like young children—in photographs, where they can't drool, scream, or squirm.

"I know my place," Judy said. "I'd never take my kids to a restaurant with wallpaper."

But they have to eat somewhere. "It's almost impossible to feed the kids and do the marketing the same day. By the time you clean the floor and change their clothes again, the afternoon is shot. That's why Dierbergs, my supermarket, is such a great place. I wouldn't take my kids into their nice restaurant, The Courtyard. But they have this little snack bar. It has hot dogs and hamburgers on paper plates. My girls can't hurt anything.

"Dierbergs is one of those supermarkets that has everything: a florist, a big video department, a post office. I can feed the kids and do all my shopping at one place.

"But lately businessmen and women have taken over my snack bar. These people can eat anywhere they want. They can go to quiet little bistros. They can eat Italian, Chinese, and Mexican. So what are they doing eating hot dogs with my girls?

"One afternoon I'm at lunch in the snack bar, reading to the girls. Their favorite character is about to be carried off in a tornado. My little girl shrieks, 'Oh, no, Mommy!' Two businesswomen turned around and glared at me.

"Another afternoon we're sitting next to two businessmen. One is making a big sale. My little girl turns and squirts mustard at his Armani suit. I almost died. Then I thought, 'No, why should I? I don't go to their places. They shouldn't go to the supermarket.'

"When I'm in a business suit, I don't go to a supermarket, except to pick up something on the way home. But when I'm a suburban mommy in knit pants, an oversized top that can't be stained any more and a tote bag crammed with diapers and complete changes of clothes in two sizes, I belong in the supermarket. That is my territory. I want it back."

I was afraid she'd hold her breath until she turned blue if I didn't have lunch at Dierbergs.

It was just as Judy said. You'd have to work hard to spend five bucks for lunch. Continental subs, bagel dogs, and cheese nachos didn't look like power food. But at 12:15, all but one of the white metal tables were filled with gray suits, beige raincoats, and sincere ties.

There were young women in bow ties, gray-haired executives in yellow ties, and one high-powered type in a bright red tie lunching with an elegant woman in silk and leather.

Over the rattle of grocery carts you could hear phrases like: "that Mark Twain deal" . . . "20 to 25 percent" . . . "I think we could be close to coming out competitive."

At one table, the dealing got rough. "I want a marshmallow," said a little girl firmly. She was a tough cookie in red leotards and Mary Janes.

"I have some orange sections," said Mom, a pushover in pink. "They're nice orange sections. Can you say 'section'?"

"Marshmallow!" said the kid.

She was the only child there. Judy was right. The business types had taken over. I asked the two suits sitting across the aisle what they were doing here. Why weren't they at a real restaurant?

"We tried," said Eric Ausubel. He works for a nearby computer sales firm. "First we went to a steak house, but it was temporarily closed. Then we went to the Mexican restaurant across the street, but it had a long line. The Courtyard had a big wait, too. So we came to the snack bar. The bottom line is: It's good. It's cheap. It's fast.''

''Most of us around here have from twelve to one for lunch,'' said his lunch partner, Phil Cagney. ''We don't have any other time to eat. We'll make a deal with the mom. If she'll bring the kids at eleven or after one, we'll promise not to bother her.''

You better hope Judy accepts your deal, Phil. Because if she ever unleashes those kids, you'll learn the real meaning of Quality Time.

50. City Crime and Suburban Pranks

When you live in the city, you think it's the only place with any excitement. The suburbs seem bland as baby food.

That's not true. Let me tell you a story of suburban loss, suffered by a young girl. We'll call her Paula.

Paula's mother printed her sad story in a newsletter she sends out in her West County suburb. A woman who got the newsletter sent it to me with this letter.

''Does your heart go out to daughter Paula?'' she wrote. ''How does this family deal with such a loss?''

Here's what the newsletter said:

''Sometime Saturday night, July 16th, or early Sunday morning, a radar detector was removed from my daughter's car.

''Because of the circumstances surrounding the theft, the belief of the authorities and ourselves is that someone in the neighborhood is responsible.

''While I know that teenagers and even younger children do participate in pranks and dangerous stunts, this is of even far greater circumstance.

''Paula's Porsche was parked in the back yard, and we live on a cul-de-sac. Not just anyone goes through there. Usually it's only neighbors. Again, because of the other item missing, the authorities believe this was more a lark and a prank than an actual theft.

''But this is where you as a parent may be of assistance. We are willing not to pursue any prosecution with the return of the detector.

''NO QUESTIONS ASKED.

''If we must, we will further continue working with the authorities and when the detector is found, we will make sure that we prosecute to the fullest and make the person responsible pay for this folly.

''Again, I would rather have the detector back, no questions asked.

''Please check with your children. Ask them if they have heard anything or if they know anything about it. I think we as adults sometimes underestimate just what all our children know, and our children do not tell us as parents simply because they know we'll be shocked or can't deal with their 'real world.' But that's another subject entirely.

"Help me out with this, please. And also if you have had things disappear, let me know. We may have something started that needs mass involvement from the community.

"I know I can count on you to inquire from your children (sic). Someone knows about it, and I'm sure is bragging about it."

Paula's radar detector is no small loss. They cost between $100 and $250. Two months after the event, Paula's mother still had no word about the fate of the Fuzzbuster or the mysterious "other item."

"We've had no news," she said. "Nothing. Paula had the keys in her car, and they also took the Porsche emblem off the key chain. We've had other pranks in the neighborhood. I learned a house was TP'd and shaving creamed. So it may have been kids."

Paula's mother also said a street crew was working in the subdivision, but I wasn't sure whether they were suspects or victims.

But I don't always understand suburban language. When a city kid swipes something over $100, we call that a crime. In the suburbs, it's a prank.

Because the suburbs aren't crime-ridden like the city, people don't have to lock everything up. Some feel so safe, they even leave the keys in their Porsches. This causes more pranks.

I was in over my head. I needed a suburban person to translate the newsletter for me. I asked my West County expert, Lauren Davis, for help.

"The most important words in that story are 'No Questions Asked,' " Lauren said. "Those three words are the suburban motto. They mean, 'I want my stuff back.'

"City people want revenge. The suburbs know what's important— property. Besides, it wouldn't do any good to prosecute these kids. Their parents' lawyers would get them off. Then all their friends would come back and give you lawn jobs."

A lawn job is when a young person drives onto your grass, hits the gas, and leaves deep ruts.

"Another threat to your property," Lauren explained.

But if no questions were asked, why wasn't the Fuzzbuster returned?

"Whoever took it, wanted it for their car," said Lauren. "They stole it for a reason. They're using it. By now, it's probably been stolen out of that car. It could have been on three or four cars already. It's probably making the rounds of West County."

That's the nice thing about the suburbs. The fun-loving kids are so busy with pranks, they don't commit crimes like city kids.

51. How to Read a Real Estate Ad

It took David Riassetto three years to find a new house. When the search was over, it left him with one strange side effect.

"I still like to read the real estate ads," David said. "I can't help myself. They use a different language. Now that I've learned it, I don't want to lose it. So I read the ads and try to figure out what they're really saying."

David has learned well. I checked his translations with a St. Louis real estate agent, Diane Freer. Right now, her life is just ducky. So is every other real estate agent's.

"Half the houses in St. Louis have country duck decor," Diane said. "That means wreaths on the door and ducks everywhere. White ducks with yellow ribbons on blue wallpaper. A few geese are optional."

Diane added her own favorites to David's list. Thanks to Diane and David I can give you:

A Real Real Estate Guide

A quarter of a century old: So are you. At least. This phrase gives new dignity to an ordinary ranchburger in an area with interesting older homes.

Close to the city: As in Kansas City.

Close to the interstate: The highway is ten feet from your backyard.

Close to the schools: The kids cut through your yard.

Close to shopping: You're ten feet from the mall. The traffic clogs your street.

Contemporary executive home: The neighborhood is overpriced. The house is done in trendy colors that will go out of style as soon as you move in.

Cream puff: You don't have to wash the windows when you move in.

Cute: Country duck decor.

Dry basement: It used to be wet. If the owners had any sense, they'd keep their mouths shut, but they paid $4,000 to have it fixed and they want you to know it.

Fabulous: A 1950s house with a new kitchen.

Handyman's dream: Your nightmare.

Historic older home for renovation: If you're a contractor with $500,000 to spend.

Ideal for Dinks: It sounds like an insult, but it isn't. A Dink is a "double income, no kids" couple. "Ideal for Dinks" means the house is too small and inconvenient for anyone else. And the neighborhood may be questionable.

Motivated seller: Nobody wants the place. It's been on the market eight months.

Only fifteen minutes from downtown: At 2 A.M. on Sunday.

Ready to move in: Lord knows what the owners are trying to hide.

Renovated kitchen with modern built-ins: Expensive appliances you'll use twice, at the move-in and move-out parties.

Short drive to the city. Also, **located in the country:** In the sticks.

Stunning cedar contemporary: Hanging off the side of a cliff, with a stunning view of the interstate.

Stunning multi-level contemporary: Lots of steps.

Stunning: The kitchen is less than ten years old.

52. Cruising: It Ain't Just Driving Around

I don't know what you called it, but at my high school it was cruising. You know, carloads of teenage girls would drive around looking for guys. Meanwhile, carloads of guys were driving around looking for girls. The cruising route was as regular as a bus line: Circle Steak 'n Shake, buzz the highway strip, hit McDonald's, the park and finally back to Steak.

As you drove around, you hung out the car windows and waved and yelled. The guys would wave and yell back. Nothing much else happened.

There were rumors about wild goings on in parks and quarries. But nobody I knew ever met a boy cruising, except Sandy, who wore green eye shadow and was wild. Sandy said she met a cute guy at Steak 'n Shake, and they necked in his Mustang. Sandy wore a chiffon scarf around her neck for a week, claiming to hide a hickey.

No one believed her.

All this belongs to the incredibly distant past, and would have stayed there, except that a suburban woman named Karen called with some important news. Cruising is not dead. The younger generation is still carrying on this fine tradition.

"I'm twenty-five and I work at an office with two teenage girls, seventeen and eighteen," Karen said. "They're just out of high school and they still go cruising. Last week they took me along. It's a little different— the route's not so regular now—but it's all right. You ought to come along with us to see."

The date was set for Thursday night. The cruising party was to meet at 7:30 in a drugstore parking lot. Karen showed up first, wearing jeans and a yellow T-shirt with a green frog on it that said, "I'm so happy I could just shit."

"I'll wear it inside out if anyone objects," she offered.

Pam and Allison, the two teenage cruisers, arrived shortly afterward. Girls who go cruising are always named Pam and Allison. Pam had a thin elfin face, brown-blond hair piled on top her head, and plucked eyebrows. She wore the cruising uniform: T-shirt, jeans and Dr. Scholl's sandals. Allison varied the standard outfit slightly with tennis shoes, and her shoulder-length hair hung loose. Otherwise she looked about like Pam.

Allison and Pam were both cute, the highest teenage accolade. But even more important, they were cruising in Allison's brand-new sports car, a white Firebird Esprit with orange and red stripes, spoiler, bucket seats, fire-engine red interior—and a T-top. T-tops are specially suited for cruising. You can really lean out the windows and yell.

"A car like this gets the guys," Pam said. "You've got to go cruising in the right car. The right car may even be more important than the guy. I mean, if I saw a cute guy in an ugly car, I'd have to think about it. Firebirds, Camaros, Corvettes—any kind of sports car—are cruising cars."

The two old folks, Karen and I, folded ourselves into the back seat. Pam and Allison sat up front. Allison drove. Pam played the radio, switching stations to skip the news and commercials and find the best music: Billy Joel, Rolling Stones, Jackson Browne and Allison's favorite song, Joe Walsh's "Life's Been Good." The cruisers all sang it: "My Maserati does one-eighty-five. I lost my license and now I can't drive."

The radio was so loud you didn't hear the music, you felt it. The wind whipped through the T-top and snapped your hair like a flag on a windy day. It was a good feeling.

Pam explained the basic cruising rules. "We hang out the windows, whistle and yell 'Hey Babe.' But if the guys start to follow, we panic and run off."

"Sometimes," said Allison.

"First we're heading into Illinois to Ed's for beer," said Karen, who acted as interpreter. At that time, the drinking age was nineteen in Illinois. "Then we cross back into Missouri for the rest of the cruising."

Ed's was in Illinois, but just barely—it practically sat on the bridge approach. Ed's was an unpainted cinder-block building. The parking lot was filled with white rock and potholes. Big signs on the roof advertised Ice Cold Beer.

Inside, Ed's was stripped to the bare essentials: Beer stacked in cases and packed in coolers. The cruisers decided on three 8-packs of 7-ounce baby Miller's. It was wishful thinking. Everyone barely finished one beer.

The cashier asked for my driver's license. The cruising party had the grace not to laugh until we got back on the highway.

It was 8:10 when we rolled out of Ed's in a cloud of dust and went back over to Missouri. Pam passed out the beer, Allison offered cigarettes, Karen had gum.

"On to Brazilia Apartments, the home of the foxes," Allison said.

"God, there are some nice looking guys there. Nice dark bodies."

We circled the Brazilia parking lot, but nothing much was happening. Pam and Allison yelled "Hey Babe" at some nicely tanned guys sitting around the Brazilia pool, but they had to admire them from afar. We were separated by a high fence.

The next stop was Forest Park. We drove along the section past the Art Museum, where the handsome young men sat by their cars, meeting other handsome young men. Pam and Allison yelled, "What a waste!"

"They're all so good-looking," mourned Karen. "It's worse than priests."

Allison headed west on Highway 40, toward suburban Clayton "and the rich guys."

A carload of boys roared by, waving and yelling. "AALLLL RIGHT!" Allison said. "We got a 'Hey Babe!' Write that down."

Hey Babe is a compliment, Karen explained. Gong is an insult. "There's no ten-point rating system, like in the old days, when a really cute guy got a ten, a so-so guy was a five and poor was two. Now it's just Gong and Babe."

But that night there was a real shortage of guys, both Gong and Babe.

"What a drag," said Allison. "Let's make a pit stop. Then we've got to hunt up some action. We'll drive around McDonald's, then try the side streets."

"Where are all the guys?" cried Pam. The atmosphere was grim. McDonald's yielded only a fat, bearded guy in a Chevy. "Ugh, what a gorilla!" said Pam. "He's so greasy he slides out of the seat. Besides, there's a girl with him."

Pam wanted to try the ball park. "Khoury League parks are good places. Remember the other night when we had all sorts of guys following us: guys in vans and Camaros and Corvettes. It was great." In cruising, the other night is always the good one.

"This is typical for a Thursday," said Karen. "Most cruising nights, nothing happens. On good nights you yell at cute guys. On fantastic nights you actually meet one."

We stopped at another McDonald's, this time for food. Then it was back in the car. "Hey Babe, I'm in love," Allison yelled at a curly-haired boy in a baseball suit. That was the last sighting for a long time. Pam and Allison decided the only way to get some excitement was to drive through the grounds of the Paraclete Fathers.

"It's real spooky," Allison said. "The roads are so narrow you can't turn around. There are weird houses with crazy priests in them and a cross that drips blood. Dobermans snarl and jump out at you."

The road was narrow and unpaved. The trees hung down to the car top, the bushes reached out for the door handles. The radio played eerie organ music. We passed through stone gate posts.

"Far out," whispered Pam.

"Faaaantastic," said Allison.

"Check it out," said Karen. "I'm scared."

All three looked delighted, especially when we passed a castle-like stone house with one light on in the upper window. Eventually we wound up on a service road to the highway, without seeing the dripping cross or the Dobermans.

By 11:30 we were cruising on South Lindbergh, complaining about the lack of action, when Allison suddenly leaned out the window and moaned, "Ohhhhh, I'm in love." The object of her affections was a tanned, muscular guy of about twenty-five in a Grand Prix. Allison followed his car into a Fina station, yelling, "Oh, Baby, come out and play. It's Thursday night and I'm hot."

The guy in the Grand Prix stared straight ahead.

"What do you need?" asked the station attendant, sternly.

"I need him," said Allison, pointing to the Grand Prix.

"Oh Baby, Oh Baby, come out!!!" Allison yelled out the window, then turned to Pam and Karen. "My God, I hope he ain't a skink. He is good looking, isn't he?"

Allison's true love refused to budge. Finally she drove off, disgusted. Only when we were back on the street did the guy get out of the Grand Prix.

"Oh, no, his underwear top is showing out of his jeans. He's a skink. How crude," said Allison, falling out of love.

"Crrruuuude!" intoned Pam and Karen.

At the stoplight, we had a close encounter. We were in the left-turn lane when a carload of four guys pulled up next to us. "Where are you girls going?" asked the driver, a tanned, skinny blond in his early 20s. "We're going to Hondo's. Wanna join us?"

"It's Thursday night and I'm hot," yelled Allison, over the radio.

"Got any beer?" asked Pam.

"No," said the guy. "We're going to bars. Come with us."

"I've got to make a left," said Allison.

"You can cut in front of us," said the guy.

"No, we'll meet you there in half an hour."

The light changed, the guys drove off, and we made our left turn. "Are we going to meet them?" asked Pam.

"No," said Allison. "What can I say? He's a dog."

Once again, nothing happened. That's cruising. The evening was nearly over, except for a brief panic when it looked as if a police officer was following us—"Quick, hide the beer under the seat"—and a drive down the twisting, deserted Christopher Drive, where someone trotted out the old Body-in-the-Car story. You've heard a variation of this legend. A Corvette (Firebird, T-Bird) is for sale for $75 because a body had been in the trunk for three months. The car is always in perfect condition. Except for that odor.

Allison made one more tour of the Brazilia Apartments at midnight. "The home of the foxes" was even deader than the first time. In fact, the whole city was shut up tight.

"There's not much you can do at their age," Karen explained. "Pam and Allison are too young for discos, except on kiddie nights, and too young for bars. What's left except cruising?"

Allison headed down the highway toward home. Her Firebird was passed by a white Rally Sport Charger.

"Oh, no, it's driven by a GIRL . . . with an OLD LADY PASSENGER," said Allison.

Frantic with rage and shame, Allison stomped down hard on the gas and tried to catch up with the Charger. Racing ninety miles an hour through the traffic, she still couldn't catch it.

"The Charger's got a 350 engine and I've only got a 305," she said through gritted teeth.

"Stop!" I yelled at last, proclaiming myself a coward and a killjoy. Allison only went faster.

"That won't work," said Karen. "You have to yell this: Cop!!"

Karen knew the magic word. Allison slowed down. The driver of the Charger flipped us the finger and roared on. It was back to the drugstore parking lot in defeat. The cruise was over at 1:30. Six hours, and we didn't get anywhere.

"My Baby's coming home Saturday," said Allison. "No more cruising then. Just parking."

53. I Can't Live Without Them

"Are you going to leave the South Side?" she asked.

Behind the polite question, I could hear the impolite one: "You're doing OK now. Why are you living in an old walkup city flat, when you can afford a nice house in a fancy suburb like Ladue?"

"I'm staying on the South Side," I said. "I couldn't live in Ladue. It doesn't have alleys."

City or suburb, everyone lives behind a facade. The neat streets and lawns rarely reveal the muddled lives inside.

Only alleys admit what goes on behind the facade: sex, death, decay, and the offbeat beauty of everyday life.

Alleys reveal life's dark side, little by little. They keep you from growing up too sheltered.

Alleys are where you choked on your first cigarette, smoked your first joint, saw your first dirty words spelled on the walls.

Alleys kept you quick, smart, and strong. City kids played in alleys, but you had to be on the lookout for speeding cars. If you couldn't spare a kid to stand lookout, you constructed crafty barricades to slow the cars.

Alleys may have been kids' playgrounds, but for adults, they were an alternative street system. When the main streets were clogged with traffic, or sometimes, just for the hell of it, real city slickers could find their way home through the alleys.

I once knew a guy who didn't want to stand in the long lines at City Hall for his city sticker. No one did. But the morning after the sticker deadline, the cops staked out all the neighborhood stop signs, and ticketed you on your way to work.

The guy drove a big, gold Chrysler about the size of a living room, so you'd think he'd be an easy target.

He wasn't.

For six weeks, his tires never touched a city street. He kept to the alleys. When the heat was off, he went down to City Hall, bought a late city sticker, and proudly drove home, a free and honest citizen.

He knew his alleys.

Alleys are where you get another education. That's where city kids learn about sex. Thanks to stray dogs, nightwailing cats and carelessly

opened bedroom windows on Saturday afternoons, you knew as much as most farm kids. And you didn't have to look at a cornfield, either.

Alleys gave you a sense of history. You could see the city's story in layers, like an archaeologist, thanks to the patched and potholed alleys. At the bottom was the old red brick from horse and buggy days. Then asphalt, for the cars. And if you lived in a rich neighborhood, the city topped that with a layer of concrete. You saw crumbling ashpits, planted with sunflowers and climber roses, that belonged to the days when city people could still burn their trash and leaves.

You also learned early that everyone wasn't safe and friendly. When I was six, we lived in an older suburb that had a few alleys behind the local shopping strip.

I was on an important errand: taking my mother's deposit envelope to the bank. I had my five-year-old brother with me. This was another important responsibility, a sign that I was almost grownup.

We left in a flurry of parental advice: Keep your sweater on. Stay on the sidewalk. Don't talk to strangers or take rides from anyone. So much advice seemed overdone. The bank was only two blocks away, if we took a short cut through the alley.

In the alley, standing by a store dumpster, was a strange man. He stepped forward, reaching for my little brother and saying in an oddly quiet voice, "Come here, little boy."

I stood there, tightly clutching the five-year-old's hand, and said in a prissy but firm voice, "No! You can't have him! He's my little brother."

The man stood there, laughing and laughing, while we ran away.

I can still hear his laughter in my dreams, mocking and insistent, a reminder that craziness lurks in the world, waiting to destroy your life.

Alleys were where you got beat up by your first bully. In the crazy, criminal code of childhood, you never squealed. You licked your wounds in silence, and decided whether you were going to beat them, join them, or find a new system where you had another choice.

I felt sorry for kids who never had an alley education. I knew a woman—bright, witty, well-dressed. She had the best education at eastern schools. She should have had some of the worst education in the alleys. Maybe then she would have never had an unfortunate affair with a good old boy.

He demeaned her in every way. He laughed at her education, saying she had no common sense. He laughed at her sophisticated clothes, and said she dressed like a witch. He made fun of her feminist causes, and said women were flighty. He made sure her friends and coworkers knew about their affair in humiliating ways. He did everything but show the sheets around the office.

She thought this slob was honest and funny. She didn't realize he was insulting her—in her society insults were more subtle. She thought he was joking when he said those outrageous things.

But he meant every word.

If she'd hung out in alleys, she would have known a bum when she saw one.

There were real bums in the alley. Along with street people, trash pickers, and plain old scavengers. If you ever looked in your own alley, you didn't believe the smug politicians who said the poor were too lazy to work.

We saw the proud poverty of old women on fixed incomes. They lived in good neighborhoods, and they would rather die than take charity. In the twilight and early morning, you would find them, thin, gray and rustling like rats as they went through the supermarket dumpsters for stale bread and vegetables with soft spots.

There were the homeless, trundling down the alleys with their stolen grocery carts, looking for aluminum cans, liberating copper gutters from the sides of houses. They were after anything they could turn into cash.

There were the freebooters, who preferred nights on a cold park bench to the daily grind of a dull job. One I'll call Mitch roamed our neighborhood for years, carrying a plastic milk jug containing a clear liquid that looked like water but probably wasn't.

The neighborhood women gave him a wide berth, but except for an occasional loud outburst at a liquor store, Mitch never bothered anyone.

Rumor said he lived on what he scavenged, plus a few handouts and the small change he earned sweeping up for a neighborhood store.

Mitch had a shaved head and powerful muscles. He never wore a coat. Even in the coldest weather, he wore cut-off pants with a flap cut in the seat.

One cold winter, the women at the neighborhood bakery took pity on Mitch, his bare legs nipped by the cold, his rear end flapping in the breeze. They chipped in and bought him a good pair of khaki workpants at Sears.

The next day, they saw Mitch in the new khakis. The pants legs were cut off above the knees, and there was a fresh-cut flap in the back.

Some people scavenged in the alley for the sheer joy of finding something for nothing. The best alley scavenger I knew picked up a new vacuum cleaner that way. The owner had put it out for the trash after it quit working. The only thing wrong was some paper blocking the air hose.

Don H. found a pretty good typewriter by an alley trash can. He took it to a typewriter repair shop. The man at the shop asked him where he found it.

''In the alley,'' said Don H. All the store employees burst out laughing, while Don H. stood there looking puzzled.

Finally, the man behind the counter explained. His father, the store's founder, was a city boy who had this scheme to increase business: He wanted to leave broken typewriters in the alleys. People would find them and bring them into his shop to get them fixed.

His sophisticated suburban children talked him out of the idea. They said it was too crazy. They knew no one would pick up the typewriters.

There was nothing in an alley.

54. It's Not Stealing If You Take It From a Used Car Dealer

"I've been in this game since 1972," Pat said. "I've never seen our side win yet."

Pat sells used cars in St. Louis. In case you think the wily car salesman wins every time, let Pat tell you about the Great Gas Cap Game.

"To become a participant," Pat said, "you have to lose your gas cap. Just buy gas at either a full- or self-service station. At a full-service station, a new attendant may forget to replace the cap. You can also lose it yourself at a self-serve."

"Once you notice the gas cap is gone, you have to get a new one," Pat said. "Going to the parts store is too easy. That's no challenge."

Instead, you head for a used car lot.

The game is most often played on Sunday. But some prefer the early evening hours in summer, when there's still plenty of light.

There's only one rule. "The players make sure the used car lot is closed. Then they look for the make and model they own, and swipe the gas cap."

Don't they ever get caught?

"Never. The thefts come in waves. I can almost tell when a local gas station hires a new attendant."

Who plays?

"The people who look honest. Middle-class, middle-income people from your local area. Your next-door neighbor. It's not the teenagers. It's too bad, but we watch them. We don't let suspicious types near the cars."

Unless the game is played on an official field, it doesn't count. "Some people go to a shopping center for a gas cap. But that's a different game. It's called stealing. It's not stealing if you take it from a car dealer. The rules are different for us."

Players should not expect a perfect score the first time. "Sometimes, in haste, the player may grab a cap that doesn't fit. Players may wind up with two or three extra caps before they find one that's right. Others upgrade, and take a gas cap from a newer car."

Pat says the Gas Cap Game is minor league. Skilled players swipe

radio knobs, cigarette lighters, and other interior widgets.

"As a car ages and those things disappear, they are almost impossible to replace," Pat said. "This is a more creative game. The car lot has to be open. The player may have to take a demonstration drive under the watchful eye of the sales person. Players remove any knobs they need during the drive.

"The Cigarette Switch needs advance preparation. The elements burn out on those old cigarette lighters. The player pockets his defective lighter and makes the switch while he's shown the car. He takes the good lighter and leaves the bum one behind."

But this still isn't the big league. "There are dealerships where the sales person doesn't go with you on the demo drive. Those are the ones that attract the masters—The Borrowers."

They take the whole car.

"One guy was stuck waiting while the dealer's repair shop worked on his car. He asked if he could drive a demo. He took the car out. He was gone half an hour. The dealer was getting nervous.

"Finally, the man brought back the car. He said, 'I'm not interested,' picked up his repaired car, and left.

"The dealer checked the demo. Inside was a sack of empty White Castle boxes. The customer used the demo to drive himself to lunch."

55. Confessions of an Ex-Fashion Writer

When I graduated from college, I offered the *Post-Dispatch* a real bargain: Woodward AND Bernstein, rolled into one.

The Post hired me, all right. As a fashion writer.

I had two qualifications: I was a woman and I wore clothes.

That first one almost undid me. During my interview, the editor asked a question that is now illegal. He said: "Are you planning to have children?"

I fixed him a sorrowful look and said: "Oh, sir. I'm sterile."

He blushed to his hair roots. And since he was going bald, they went pretty far back. Then he patted me on the hand. "There, there, dear," he said. "Medical science has made many advances."

And so my fashion career started, based on the first of many misunderstandings.

I was writing fashion in the dreaded jersey era. This was the early 1970s, when dresses, especially evening dresses, were made of clinging jersey.

Jersey shows every mole, bump and nipple. Especially nipple. If a nipple got into the newspaper, strong male editors would scream and faint.

We even had an editor whose title was assistant nipple chipper. Not officially, of course. He worked in the society section. But if one of the high editors thought he saw a nipple, and it was too late to remake the picture, the nipple chipper had to run down to the composing room and literally chisel the offending nipple off the metal.

That way, the public didn't see a nipple in the newspaper. They saw a gray blob that looked like someone had gorped on the woman's dress.

It wasn't easy being a fashion writer in the jersey era. My stories had to show the fashionable new dresses. Most were cut so the model couldn't wear a bra. She also couldn't show a nipple.

The solution was to have the models wear Band-Aids. That just about covered the subject for many models, anyway. But I admired those women. Ripping off that Band-Aid was incredibly painful.

Still, I didn't offer to kiss it and make it better.

When the models were made up for fashion shoots, they looked beautiful. They were also beautiful in real life. The only comfort I had was that they were miserable while they worked.

Not only did they have Band-Aids on their breasts, their sleeves were stuffed with scratchy tags, their shoe soles were protected with slippery masking tape—and for instant tailoring, their outfits were pulled back with wooden clothes pins.

From behind, the clothes pins traveled up their spines like wooden vertebrae.

In the oven-hot St. Louis summers, they had to wear heavy wool and fur fall fashions. In the bitter cold, they had to be photographed in thin summer clothes.

And not shiver, sweat or look unhappy.

I never envied them.

I didn't envy me, either.

There were other traps awaiting me. The *Post* changed fashion writers then the way you change socks. Some of these young women were free spirits, indeed.

After I was hired, I showed up at a snooty store and introduced myself to the fashion coordinator as the new fashion writer.

She looked me up and down and said, "Well, at least you wear shoes."

I couldn't figure out what the old bat meant. Later I discovered one fashion writer wore the latest "gypsy" style from New York—and showed up for an interview at the store barefoot.

Some of my troubles, I made for myself. Like the time I ran off to cover the Jean Patou trunk show, without checking the files for background on the designer.

"And how is Mr. Patou?" I asked the company representative, chummily.

"Dead for thirty years," she said, at her iciest. She was almost as cold as Mr. Patou.

At least I picked up the fashion lingo quickly.

When it was a dull season, I wrote stories about "the return of the classics."

When it was an incredibly dull season, I wrote: "Thank goodness designers are making real clothes for real women."

What were the other clothes for? Unreal women?

Actually, yes. Models in the early seventies were emaciated. Human coat hangers.

If they had generous figures, they would detract from the clothes. One of the strangest sights was backstage at a New York showing. The models were rushing around changing, when a TV crew came through.

Here was a roomful of young women with gorgeous bony faces, wearing only sheer-to-the-waist panty hose. The all-male camera crew didn't give them a second look. They treated them like the coat hangers they were.

It was a New York show that ended my fashion career. I went to New York for the spring and fall shows. Each season had its own color. That fall, I saw 3,000 plum dresses. Next spring it was 3,000 navy dresses.

And the next fall, another 3,000 dresses. The announcer came up to the podium and said dramatically, "This year, Oscar de la Renta believes in gray."

I was the only one in the room who laughed. I knew it was time for a change.

56. Make Like a Tree and Leave

In late fall, as the last leaves drop from the trees, there's a strange ritual in my city neighborhood. If you're lucky, you'll see something like this. I swear it happened:

First, the woman raked the leaves in her yard into a big pile. Then she filled two plastic bags and dumped them in the trash.

Now comes the strange part. The woman put the rest of the leaves into a big box. She tiptoed over to the fence. She looked both ways. Then she dumped the leaves into her neighbor's yard.

What are you doing, ma'am?

"I'm giving him back his leaves," the city woman said. "They fell off his tree and blew into my yard. I raked them up and threw them back. They belong to him."

Won't the leaves blow back into your yard again?

"No," the city woman said. "The wind carries them over into my yard when they come off the tree. Once they're on the ground, my fence keeps them out."

Aren't you afraid you'll get caught?

"I put two bags in the dumpster first. Then I can truthfully say I put my leaves in the trash. Besides, I wait until he goes to work with his little briefcase. He doesn't come home until late at night. He won't notice. He never rakes his yard. A few more leaves won't matter."

Why are you picking on him?

"It's not just me. Our whole block gives him his leaves back. They're scattered everywhere. And it just doesn't happen on my street. This is going on in neighborhoods all over the city."

The city old-timers all do it. They won't dump back leaves if the person is old or sick. Or if they like them. Leaf dumping is reserved for those minor city irritants: Smug yuppie couples who never bother to learn the neighborhood customs. And rehabbers who work on their houses before 7 A.M. on weekends.

The city woman glared at the yuppie's yard. "We don't grow trees—he does," she said. "He doesn't know enough to rake up after himself. His leaves blow all over. Darned yuppie."

The city woman thinks Joyce Kilmer is a sap. Forget the poetic babbling about never seeing a "poem lovely as a tree."

On the ultra-practical South Side, a tree, like everything else in this life, is a responsibility. It must be cared for and cleaned up after. Responsible tree owners are like the elderly woman on my block. She gets up at six every morning and rakes her yard. Then she thoughtfully picks off any loose leaves on the lower branches, so they won't blow into her neighbors' yards.

"Don't get me wrong," the city woman said. "We like trees. We just don't like the leaves they drop. Or the seeds and sticker balls.

"Trees drip sap on your car. Half the time, my yuppie neighbor doesn't park under his own tree. So we have to park there and get the sap on our cars.

"Trees bring birds. That's more stuff dropped on your car. And the roots raise the concrete sidewalks.

"If he wants trees, he should clean up after them, and not inflict them on everyone else. Those leaves are his property. He's letting his property blow all over the neighborhood."

Take that, yuppie. And remember this old South Side saying: If God wanted you to get shade from a tree, He wouldn't have invented the aluminum awning.

57. The Day the Church Lady Got Probation

She never did it herself. She didn't like it.

But she didn't think it should be illegal. After all, it gave some women pleasure. And let them make a little money on the side.

And that's how the Church Lady wound up on probation. She ran a charity bingo game for her suburban Catholic church.

The Missouri law's been changed, but back in 1971, bingo was a felony. Any person who organized, helped out, advertised, or called out I-29 and B-17 was risking two to five in the state pen.

Most local police departments turned a blind eye to church bingo. They might run in an occasional elderly poker player, but they bought the sentimental idea that granny gamblers were cute and harmless. Anyone who ever watched those wily old sharks in action knew they were far from toothless.

One city church bingo game was raided regularly. A parishioner complained, and the police had to act on it. Before the police arrived, someone at the stationhouse would call the church rectory and say, "Tell the ladies to sit on their bingo cards and start singing. We're on our way." By the time the police arrived, the bingo players would be singing hymns.

But there was no salvation for the Church Lady.

"Yes, I have a police record," she said. She was embroidering a shirt for one of her four boys while we talked in the family living room.

"I hate bingo. I wouldn't play it. To me, bingo is a boring evening. But it's a money maker and the old ladies love it."

So along with helping out at church picnics and cleaning up after club meetings, the Church Lady ran the bingo game in the parish hall.

"I won't tell you the name of the parish, because the pastor got in so much trouble with the bishop, there's no point in raking it up again.

"We'd been running the bingo games once a week in the church hall. We got one warning, but we didn't pay much attention to it. All the parishes around here ran bingo games.

"We made about $125 on a good night. About two hundred women usually came. The crowd was over fifty, and usually over sixty-five. We charged $2 for two bingo cards and 10¢ for each additional card, and some of those women could play fifteen cards or more."

Then came that fateful day in November.

"About halfway through the evening, at 10 o'clock, I looked up the steps and I never saw so many blue uniforms in my life. There were police everywhere. They poured down the steps and sealed all the exits.

"It took me a minute to figure out what was going on. Then I realized, 'We're being raided. All these police are here to take in a bunch of old women.' I was really irritated. It was ridiculous."

The Church Lady guessed there were about twenty police officers at the raid, but the newspaper said there were only eight.

"A plainclothes policeman walked up to the caller and I knew he was going to get her. I said, 'Don't arrest this woman. I'm in charge here.'

"The policeman said, 'Don't worry lady, we'll get to you, too.' "

The police confiscated the tumbling baskets, cards, markers and other bingo paraphernalia.

"But they were lovely. I think they were embarrassed. The police even helped clean up the hall after the raid. They gave us the choice of being arrested at the station or the hall. We were arrested in the church basement. Our court date was set right there."

The bingo players weren't so nice. "Those women really harassed the police," she said. "Before the bingo players could leave they had to give the police their names and ages. Suddenly the place was filled with Cleopatras and Marilyn Monroes, and they were all twenty-one years old. Even women on two canes."

The women insulted and taunted the police with, "Why don't you arrest bank robbers instead of bingo players?"

Rumor said one officer had to arrest his own grandmother, and she yelled at him, "Why aren't you out catching crooks instead of your grandmother?"

"That story could be true," said the Church Lady, "but I don't know for sure. Most of the police had relatives at the bingo game."

Three days later, the suburban mayor and the police chief were fighting over who really pulled off the daring raid. The mayor told the papers he deserved the credit for rounding up two hundred elderly women.

But the police chief thought differently.

"No, absolutely not," he told a reporter. "I understand the mayor did show up at the raid later, after it began, but he stayed outside."

Grannies can come in all ages and sexes.

A month later, the Church Lady and the bingo caller appeared in court and pleaded guilty to operating a bingo game. The judge apologized before he gave the women one-year probationary sentences. He said he'd dismiss the charges after the probation if there were no more complaints.

And what happened to the ill-gotten gambling gains?

Let's just say the Church Lady relied on the bosom of the church.

"We were afraid the police would confiscate our money," she said. "We had $600. Every time I passed the money pile I stuffed a handful of bills in my bra. I went from a 36B to a 40C in no time."

58. So They Buried Him in the Front Lawn

I once knew a woman who wasn't sure she should wear a low-cut dress to an office party. "I'll hang it in the bathroom while I take a shower," she said. "If God wants me to wear it, He'll take the wrinkles out."

Does He do alterations, too?

Maybe that's why the world is in such rotten shape. God is too busy pressing pants and steaming dresses to work on world peace.

Now it looks as if God—or one of His associates—is selling real estate on the side. At least Mary Kirkpatrick thinks so. To sell her home, she buried a statue of St. Joseph in her front yard. Right by the For Sale sign. It sold the next day.

"I feel funny about it," Mary said. "Actually, I don't know what caused it. I just thank God the house is sold.

"I'd never heard about St. Joseph until my friend Phyllis sold her house that way. She said, 'Don't list, just bury St. Joseph.' He sells it right away, too. It's gone the next day or so.

"We had our house on the market six weeks. No one was interested. Then two people canceled appointments in one day. My husband Bob said, 'Let's bury St. Joseph. What can we lose?' "

Bob asked for the statue at a religious supply store. "The woman said, 'You're selling your house.' Just like that. She sells them by the case. She was temporarily out."

At the next store, when Bob asked for St. Joseph, "the clerk said, 'The display kind or burying kind?'

"My husband said, 'What's the difference?' "

About $4.

"The burying ones were plain tan plastic," Mary said. "They cost about 79¢."

Bob spared no expense. He bought two. "You have to bury St. Joseph upside-down, facing the street. At least, that's what Phyllis said. And if you dig up the statue before you move, you'll lose your financing."

That night after the burial, "we were sitting around the house. Since the two appointments were canceled, it wasn't cleaned up. I saw a truck come down our street. I said to my husband, 'It's for us. Start cleaning up.' He didn't believe me. I picked up the laundry off the couch and started running around. Sure enough, it was a couple to see the house. They said they were sorry. They thought they'd called ahead. They looked around and made a bid.

"The next day we had another couple. They made an even higher bid. We accepted."

Mary liked them. "The wife's grandfather came along. He picked up a penny in our driveway. He said it was a lucky penny and this was a lucky house. I thought, 'Great. Two sets of superstitions. One picks up pennies, the other buries statues. We belong together.'

"I work for a dentist who isn't Catholic. He teased me about my voodoo real estate. He went to a church meeting and told everyone. A woman who sells expensive houses told him, 'We used to laugh. We don't any more. It's odd, but it works.' "

Tradition says St. Joseph, the husband of Christ's mother, Mary, was a carpenter. It doesn't say why his 79¢ plastic image would sell $100,000

homes.

"It's a good investment," said a saleswoman at Catholic Supply of St. Louis. "A gentleman here knows a woman who couldn't sell her $400,000 house. She was afraid she'd have to come down on her price. Instead, she got St. Joseph and the house sold the next day. It's an old custom. You say a prayer and bury the statue. Afterward, you dig St. Joseph up and give him a place of honor in your new home."

Doris Mantia says St. Joseph sold her place. She works at Count Your Blessings Inc., a South County religious supply store. "I did it twenty-three years ago and it worked. I felt kind of stupid. But St. Joseph doesn't care. He sells your house without commission. He's been so overlooked for so long, and now he's finally come into something big."

Doris had her statue "blessed by the priest. Then you have to believe, or it doesn't work. Some bury St. Joseph upside-down, but I think that's cruel."

Doris sells a St. Joseph statue "an inch tall in a plastic case. It's great for burying. Only costs a dollar. Some people like to bury the $3 St. Joseph with child. It's magnetic, for car dashboards. We can't keep St. Joseph in stock. Real estate agents buy several at once."

Does the House of the Lord help out house sellers?

Mary Kirkpatrick said, "I know a real estate agent who keeps the statues in her purse and secretly buries them. My neighbor is a non-believer. She said, 'We sold our house last year and we didn't need St. Joseph.'

"The agent was standing right there. She said, 'I hate to tell you this, but I buried one in your yard. The house sold the next day.' "

59. The Epitaph Is a Dying Art

Gayle Gibson was walking through a suburban cemetery, one of the newer ones with flat headstones and grass like a putting green. The place was deadly dull.

"None of the tombstones said anything interesting. In the old days, epitaphs were entertaining," Gayle said. "Now all you get are your name and your birthday. Who cares? Nobody's coming out with a cake and candles. We need more creativity."

Gayle's right. We put our most intimate thoughts on T-shirts. We have messages on everything from bumper stickers to parking meters. But our tombstones are dry as dust.

"If we're going to be there for a while, we might as well be entertaining," Gayle said. "This is our last chance to say something. We're wasting it."

Even taking it for granite.

The right epitaph can make a lasting impression. I still remember this killjoy verse I saw in the Bahamas:

"Remember man, as you pass by,
"As you are now, so once was I.
"As I am now, so must you be
"Remember, man, eternity."

A good epitaph can tickle your funny bone. A reader gave me two favorites, supposedly from nineteenth-century cemeteries:

"Owen Moore has gone away,
"Owin' more than he can pay."

Here's one, er, Moore:

"Here lies the body of Lester Moore,
"Done in by a slug from a .44.
"No Les, no more."

Modern epitaphs could be just as entertaining. I offer this sample epitaph on the grave subject of shopping till you drop:

"Her life was short, her death was hard.
"She was buried in debt by her MasterCard."

The same story could have a religious theme:

"In the midst of life we are in debt."

"I've already got my epitaph," Gayle said. " 'Proceed on.' It means they can walk on by me—or they can continue on with their life. What would you put on your tombstone?"

How about: "Out of print."

Or: "Better read than dead."

But getting your epitaph an audience could be a problem. The great age of epitaphs also was a great time for death. In those days, families used to make regular outings to the graveyards. You'd spend a cheery Sunday afternoon tending the family plot.

Today, any parent who suggested quality time at the graveyard would be packed off to the nearest shrink. My own theory is the epitaph died when people quit hanging around cemeteries. I'm happy to say a check of some monument dealers shows I'm all wet.

A woman at a St. Louis monument company said: "Tombstones with epitaphs are still allowed in older cemeteries, but the new parklike ones want flat headstones because they're easier to trim around. These are usually your commercial cemeteries. Some Catholic cemeteries have two sections. You can have a big monument, but you pay more for your lot. The flat-headstone, easy-to-care-for lots are cheaper.

"Go to the right cemetery and you can say what you want," she said. "As with most things these days, it comes down to money."

Leonard DeMoor, at the Tom Murray Monument Co., said: "General-ly speaking, people just use their name and birthday on monuments.

But there's a trend to personalize.

"We just did an unusual monument. It's for a man whose father was a friend of Charles Lindbergh. Thanks to him, the young boy became interested in aviation. So we cut a small airplane on the stone. We also put two soccer balls on the grave of a big-time coach. Another family wanted us to use as an epitaph a verse that has been read at family funeral services for generations. It's the longest epitaph I remember—490 letters."

This touching verse begins:

"Nay; do not weep or grieve for me my own,

"I shall forever be close to you all.

"And when you call, I shall be nearer God to intercede.

"Indeed, I can help you more than e'er before . . ."

More personalized monuments are "a trend I've noticed in the last couple of years," DeMoor said. "I'm glad it's changing. Sometimes, just names seems kind of cold."

But just names could be safer. Consider this 1947 story I dug out of the files. It said a young widow had this sentiment carved on her husband's tombstone: "My sorrow is more than I can bear."

Later, she remarried and had the epitaph amended. She added one more word. Now it read: "My sorrow is more than I can bear alone."

60. Would You Autograph My Door?

Can the right car change your life? It sure put Larry Balch's on a different track. Thanks to his car, Larry says he's been backstage at Beach Boys concerts and partied with Charlie Daniels.

Not bad for a guy who has a little house in the suburbs and a driveway full of beat-up cars.

"My car brings me so much attention," Larry said. "People wonder who I am. They don't know I'm nobody."

That's not true. Larry has a signed original. His car is signed by nine Beach Boys, including all the original members still alive—Brian and Carl Wilson, their cousin Mike Love, and their friend Al Jardine. Only the late Dennis Wilson's signature is missing. And there's no way Larry can get that one.

"It took me three years to get all those autographs," Larry said. Brian Wilson was the last to sign. Larry bagged him about three weeks ago in Chicago.

Larry's Beach Boy car is the same glaring yellow as a hot California sun. The color is Fiat Chrome Yellow. On top may be the only surfboard in suburban St. Louis.

The car is a '48 Chevy sedan delivery. It looks like an overgrown station wagon, with a door in the back and a great streamlined sweep of

front fenders. The side panels are painted with surfing murals. There's
another mural on the back door. They're all done by Dan Patterson of
Air Power Graphics.

But that's not the best part. The back door is signed by the Beach Boys.

Larry says he got his first three signatures before a 1985 concert in
St. Louis. Band member Bruce Johnston came out "and saw my car.
He said, 'Is that yours?'

"I thought I was in trouble. I was using their name and they were
going to sue me. Instead, Johnston walked over and said, 'That is really
neat.' Then he wrote 'The Beach Boys' on the back door and signed
his name. Al Jardine signed, too. So did Mike Love. I missed Carl Wilson.
He was late and running for his dressing room."

Larry turned the car's interior into a Beach Boys shrine. There are
framed photos of Larry with the band members. Framed backstage passes.
The seats are embroidered with the band name. Even the bar has their
signatures on it.

"It started as a joke," Larry said, "but now it's gone wild.

"I traded a '39 Chevy for this car. It had no glass in the windows,
one tail light, and an old stock six engine. It took me and my buddy
Mike O'Neal six months to fix it up. People said, 'What are you going
to put on the car?' A friend had just brought me a T-shirt from a Beach
Boys concert. I held up the shirt and said, 'This.' Everybody made fun
of me."

They quit laughing after the first set of signatures. Now Larry takes
his car to distant Beach Boys concerts and auto shows. In between, he
drives it around the city.

"Everybody trailers their show cars. I drive mine and have a good
time. It's got 185,000 miles on it. That car has been everywhere from
Texas to Chicago. Sure, I've had to do some touch-ups. People have
opened doors on it, and I've had to fix scratches. But only the signatures
are sacred. I'd hate to think what will happen to the insurance of anybody
who hits that back door."

Larry has devised some unusual protection. Under the back bumper,
flame throwers belch fire. "I can flip a switch and keep people from
tailgating.

"They caught fire the other night at Chuck-A-Burger. I was afraid
I'd burned my back door. But there was no damage."

To the car, that is.

"It did burn all the hair off a guy's legs. He was standing nearby.
I was really worried he got hurt, but the guy said it was no problem.
He liked the light show."

Speaking of show, Larry's "biggest thrill is meeting the Beach Boys."

He also says the car helped introduce him to Charlie Daniels. "I was parked by the band bus at his concert. Charlie Daniels walked out, saw the car, and invited me to party.

"When you pull out of a concert in that car, everyone thinks you're with the band. One lady jumped up and kissed the back window. Another tried to drag one of my buddies out of the car.

"You wouldn't believe the people who turn around when I go down the highway. One guy watched so hard, he ran into another car.

"I've turned down $25,000 for it. To me, it's like a kid. I've raised it up from nothing. It's not for sale. Not for $2 million.

"Well, maybe I'd sell the car for that. But not the back door."

61. After Midnight

I've heard wild stories about nightlife. Champagne and chauffeured limousines. And why the restroom is really called the powder room. (Those razor blades behind the mirror aren't for shaving your legs.)

But the strangest story comes from Whitey Herzog's Power House Nightclub at Union Station. At midnight they do the Duck Dance. You know, the dance you do at German weddings when you're drunk. The dance that's even dumber than the Hokey Pokey.

It happens only on Friday and Saturday nights, but that's bad enough.

Suddenly, the same crowd that's been dancing to Salt-N-Pepa's "Push It Good" gets down with the Duck Dance. Some ninety people are out on the dance floor, waddling around in leather miniskirts, quacking and clapping.

It's sick, I tell you.

The Duck Dance, also known as the Chicken or the Duckie Dance, is probably a European folk dance. It's migrated to cities such as Minneapolis, Chicago, and St. Louis. It's usually played at beer gardens and German weddings, but only late in the evening. Especially in St. Louis.

See, this city's real men don't like to dance. They think it's something for wimps and gigolos. So St. Louis women have to dance with each other. It looks odd to outsiders, but what are you going to do? The only way to get St. Louis men on the dance floor is to give them vast quantities of the local brew. A few more beers, and they will tackle really demeaning dances like the Hokey Pokey. And when they're absolutely blotto, they will do the Duck Dance.

The music sounds like a slightly warped polka. "Dah, dah, dah, dah, dah, dah, DAH, dah, dah, dah, dah, dah, DAH," begin the awful strains. That's the signal to form a circle. Then you quack your fingers, flap your wings, waggle your tail and clap your hands.

Naturally, with those movements, the Duck Dance can be vulgar. But when you watch your 250-pound aunts and uncles dirty dancing, it makes you want to lock yourself in a lighthouse. Alone. For a long time.

"The Duck Dance is better than a Breathalyzer test," said a man who's danced it. "It's a sure sign you're loaded. Fortunately, you only dance it at weddings."

That keeps it in the family. Dating couples only take someone they're serious about to a family wedding. In the early stages of courtship, when you're still trying to impress each other, she will keep her more rancid relatives away from the man she loves.

Relatives come out of the woodwork at weddings. He'll see Cousin Elmer, who makes soap sculptures. And Aunt Edna, who has blue hair and gold lame moccasins.

On the other hand, she's seen you Duck Dance.

Now that you have faced the worst about each other, you are ready to marry. You vow to work hard, save your money, move out of the old neighborhood, and only dance at nightclubs.

The Duck Dance at a class joint is a frightening thought. Would Fred Astaire Duck Dance? Or Mel Gibson? How can you meet someone after she's seen you waddle? How can you be debonair and Duck Dance?

Herzog's Power House is probably the only night club in town with Duck Dancing. "It has a real strong base in St. Louis," said Tammy Baker, director of marketing and promotions. "We did the Duck Dance when we had the beer garden at Union Station. Then when the Power House opened in October, it came over here.

"It's cheap aerobics. Your legs really hurt after you waddle around on the dance floor."

Up in the ultra-modern sound booth, the DJ puts on the Duck Dance record, a forty-five by Herb Eberle.

The, er, duck caller, Philip Keeler, comes out on the floor with a microphone and lets loose a flock of duck puns: "Let's get down. . . shake a tailfeather . . ."

The dance itself is led by a costumed Dorrel the Duck. Dorrel is Whitey Herzog's real name, and it's no accident that Dorrel's duck costume shows a strong Fredbird influence.

Kim Tesson is one of the people behind Dorrel the Duck.

Do you get your feet stepped on when you lead the dance, Kim?

"Yeah," she said. "I get goosed a lot, too."

62. *They Get Desperate Over a Broken Nail*

I was sitting in a St. Louis beauty shop when I heard Marlene the manicurist on the phone. She was talking to a desperate customer.

"I'm sorry," she said, in a voice as soothing as pink hand lotion. "I'm really booked this afternoon. I'm sorry you broke your nail, but the earliest I can see you is tomorrow morning.''

Marlene paused, listening to the pleas. Then she searched her appointment book, and said, ''Well, maybe I can fit you in at 2:15.'' She hung up with a sigh.

I can't believe a woman would carry on like that over a broken nail.

''It wasn't a woman,'' said Marlene. ''It was a man. My men customers are much worse than the women. You should hear some of the men when they want their nails done before a big meeting or a party.''

Most people don't even know men who get manicures. Marlene said she'd talk about them, ''if you don't use my real name. I wouldn't want to hurt their feelings. They're nice guys. Good tippers, too.''

Marlene's customers are well-heeled. ''They're doctors, lawyers, salesmen, construction company owners—real macho types. But when they get a hangnail, they come in with their fingers wrapped up in Band-Aids.

''They call me up on their car phones and go, 'Marlene, I'm desperate. I've got to see you right now. I broke a fingernail.' ''

Marlene takes pity on them. ''Men don't know what to do. A woman would file down the break. But men aren't taught to take care of their hands like women. They won't use lotion or oil—they're too manly for that. So their nails crack and split something awful.

''Here's something most people don't know: Men under stress bite their nails. Right down to the quick. I know when my men have had a bad week. They come in here with their hands in their pockets. They hide them like little boys. I say, 'Let me see your hands. You've been biting your nails.'

''Some do it after a tough business day. Others after a bad golf game. I can tell when one customer's game isn't going well. The hand protected by his golf glove is OK. The other hand looks terrible. He picks at it during the game.

''About half my men wear nail polish. Clear polish, but I tease them I'm going to put on a coat of red. Some of my nail biters have me put on a hard glaze to keep them from biting. The glaze is Fiberglas. It's so hard you can break a tooth on it. One man has weaned himself off nine nails, but he still chews one, and tries to hide it.''

Marlene says a manicure is a sign of success. ''Rich guys notice each other's nails. Before a big meeting, or when they go out of town, they'll call me up. They want to look perfect. The construction company guys want a manicure, but they don't want it to look like one or their men will laugh at them. It's not easy.''

Men get manicures about as often as women. ''Some men come every week for a manicure, some every two or three weeks. Men don't understand polish won't last forever. It chips and peels. I can get my women

to touch up their nails between manicures, but men won't be caught dead with a bottle of polish.

"You'd also be surprised at the number of men who like pedicures. Some get ingrown toenails or the callus builds up until it's painful. Others just like to be waited on hand and foot. And it gets them out of the office.

"I've had to perform all kinds of services: I've pulled out splinters and sewn on shirt buttons. One day, a guy came jogging in, and his pants were split. He hid in the bathroom while I sewed them up.

"But mostly I work on their nails. They need me. Men are more desperate because they can't do it themselves. But they want it at the last minute. They want it perfect. And they think I've got five sets of hands.

"Sometimes I want to say, 'Gimme a break.' "

But they do.

63. He Got a Million Dollars in the Mail

Robert Adams was a millionaire for a month. His broker accidentally sent him $1 million dollars in gold—through the mail.

But here's the really incredible part. The gold was picked up at the post office by his sweet white-haired mother, Irma Adams. And she left $1 million unguarded in her car for almost six hours.

But Bob's new-found wealth hasn't changed him. That's because he didn't get to keep a nickel of it.

Bob is a pharmacy manager in Lebanon, Mo. He says he became an instant millionaire through an error by PaineWebber. Here's what Bob says happened.

"It all started when I ordered 3,000 silver coins from my broker, Fred, in Overland Park, Kan. Through some kind of typing or clerical error, the order came back to me as 3,000 1-ounce gold eagles at $8.27 a piece. That was the price for silver. After I got a copy of the incorrect order, my broker called me and said, 'We made a mistake. I'll send you a correction.'

"Then I got another call from Fred. He said, 'Bob, we messed up again. They shipped the gold. Six boxes of it.' I said that was OK, I'd send it back. I'd instructed Fred to ship the silver to my office in Lebanon. I'd just send it back when I got all six boxes."

Bob lives with his mother in Osage Beach, an Ozark community about forty miles from Lebanon. "My mother called and said there were some notices in our mail box for a couple of packages and she'd pick them up.

"Then I got another phone call from Fred. He said, 'We messed up again. We shipped the gold to Osage Beach.'

"That meant my little white-haired mother had picked it up.

"I called her and said, 'Mother, did you pick up my packages?' She said, 'With a truck. I couldn't lift them. The postmaster had to carry them to the car for me.' She said they were still in the car.

"I said, 'Mother, you've got two boxes of gold coins.'

"She said, 'You come right home, Robert.'

"So I took the next day off and put the two boxes of coins in a bank safety deposit box. It took a while. Those boxes were heavy. They weighed about thirty pounds each.

"My mother said, 'What do I say at the post office if we get any more of those heavy boxes?' I said, 'Tell them they're diesel parts for your backhoe.'

"Two days later, I got another call from my mother. She said, 'You get right home. I got four more of those boxes.' "

Bob now had "2,000 troy ounces of gold coins. Coins are worth more than bullion. The ballpark figure for the whole thing came to about $1 million in gold. They shipped all that money in cardboard boxes. A couple had busted open and someone had just taped them up. I took another day off and put the coins in another safety deposit box. Then I just kind of forgot about them for a month.

"My broker called and said, 'We haven't got the gold yet.' I said, 'I haven't gotten the days off yet. I work six days a week, and if I take a day off I lose $150. I'm already out two days.'

"Fred said, 'That can be negotiated.' He also said the company would reimburse me for the safety deposit boxes I had rented."

Along with the gold, Bob got lots of free advice. "Suddenly, everybody was a lawyer. And they all said, 'Finders keepers.' Even a guy at the post office told me if it was shipped first class and I didn't order it, I didn't have to give it back."

Unfortunately, Bob's lawyer didn't agree. "He said I had to give the gold back. Besides, it wasn't mine."

And so he did. The transfer took place on a Tuesday. This time, the gold went special delivery. "PaineWebber sent one armored truck, two men from New York and three guards. And a whole mob of Osage Beach police officers came out to guard it. The men from New York counted the gold and gave me a written release."

How did you feel after you lost $1 million?

"Relieved. My mother wanted to take the money and run. But I said you couldn't run very fast. That stuff is heavy.

"Do you want to hear the rest of the story? I still didn't have my silver coins. I wanted PaineWebber to bring me the silver and we could swap. But they said they'd already mailed it.

"It came one day when I had a doctor's appointment: I was fishing with a dentist. I came back home and my mother said, 'I picked up something at the post office for you. It's in the car.' "

She had $32,000 in silver in the trunk. "She just took it upon herself to get it. I put it in a safety deposit box right away. But it didn't bother my mother at all. I guess she's used to handling big money.

"Today she said, 'Let's stop at the post office again.'

"I said, 'Mother, I think it's all over.' "

64. What's Pink and Sits on Your Lawn?

It may be the most momentous date in suburban history. Thirty years ago, the pink plastic flamingo first appeared on America's lawns. It was 1958, the same year the Chipmunks had a hit song.

Today, the chipmunk is just another cheeky rodent, but the flamingo flourishes.

Richard Waidmann grew up in the suburbs of St. Louis, but his home was a flamingo-less environment.

"We begged, but we couldn't get our parents to put them on the lawn," he said. "Then I grew up and moved back to the city, to South St. Louis, the perfect flamingo habitat."

When Richard found out 1988 was the plastic flamingo's thirtieth anniversary, "I just had to do something." He is holding "the first annual pink flamingo party."

The party will have only a paltry (or is it poultry?) four plastic lawn flamingos. "But we're having one hundred people, and they have to wear pink or bring a flamingo to get in. And we have an inflatable flamingo."

I was afraid to ask what that was.

Richard found out about the thirtieth anniversary from the nation's premier flamingo purveyor, a company called the Cat's Pyjamas in the tasteful state of New Jersey. To push plastic flamingos, they started the famous "ruin the neighborhood—stick 'em in your yard" campaign several years ago. A pair of flamingos now goes for $9.95 in their catalog. Or you can "buy 'em by the flock and save—10 pair for $89.95."

After you figure out why anyone would spend ninety bucks on plastic flamingos, you can think about all the flamingo letter openers, toothbrush holders, and toilet paper sold at $4.95 a roll.

Richard has a lot of flamingo paraphernalia. But what really caught his eye in the catalog was the $12.95 commemorative T-shirt. It says: "30th Anniversary of the Plastic Garden Flamingo as an Official Licensed Product." It's signed by the plastic flamingo's creator, Don Featherstone.

Featherstone was a tender twenty-one when he designed the flamingo for Union Products of Leominster, Mass.

Just what was his inspiration?

"Money," Featherstone said. "The company had a flat flamingo lawn ornament, but they asked me to design a three-dimensional one. I had nine years of art training. I did the duck lawn ornament, too. To get it right, I lived with a real duck for six months. I fed it. Cleaned up after it. Next I did the flamingo, but I couldn't have a live one at my home. I worked from pictures, including some from the *National Geographic*."

He noticed right away the flamingo was not a duck.

"The flamingo was graceful and semi-exotic. People wanted them to dress up their yards. A bare lawn is like an empty coffee table. It needs to be decorated."

Union Products also turns out pelicans and penguins and swan planters. Here's a secret: Swans and ducks outsell the flamingo. "But they don't get the same attention," Featherstone said. "People talk about the rebirth of the flamingo. It never died. Ninety-two percent of ours are bought by people who like them. Our flamingo sales have only jumped eight percent since the silliness started. That eight percent is what the media noticed. It's only the tip of the iceberg."

But it's prompted the party in South St. Louis. "I'm honored. I hope they'll play flamingo croquet at the party. You can spread the wire legs and use the flamingos for wickets."

Do you make the plastic birds into croquet mallets?

"No, the necks are too short for a good game," Featherstone said. "I was invited to one party given by a group called something like the International Club for the Preservation of the Pink Plastic Lawn Flamingo. I thought it was going to be the largest collection of yuppies in America.

"It wasn't. It was a great party. They had a bubble machine pouring out pink bubbles. There were pink spotlights, a full orchestra, a giant custom-made neon flamingo and Porta-Potties with pink flamingo toilet paper."

Featherstone has heard of flamingo fan clubs. "And a wedding where the bride and groom had one of my plastic flamingos sticking out of an $800 wedding cake. I had to wonder why.

"I don't understand what it is about flamingos. I've never seen a wedding cake with a duck on it. I know ducks are messy, but that doesn't explain the flamingo cult."

Featherstone modestly says he didn't invent the lawn flamingo. "They've been around for some time. I have cast-iron ones from 1910. The rich could afford expensive lawn ornaments.

"But my pink plastic flamingo brought poor taste to the poor folk."

65. For Mature Adults Only

It's as inevitable as death and taxes—only worse. Much worse. You know those two will get you. This strikes when you least expect it.

Just when you're feeling grown up, you get a letter from AARP. That's the American Association of Retired Persons. AARP sends out membership letters to people at age fifty.

Retired? You're in your prime. Every bit as sexy as Robert Redford or Jane Fonda, and they're both fifty. No snickering, Baby Boomers. You'll get yours in about ten years.

Paul says an AARP letter is the worst thing that happened to him since Uncle Sam said "Greetings." He got his three weeks before his fiftieth birthday.

"I didn't feel bad about turning fifty," Paul said. "This is the age when you finally get rid of the kids and the mid-life crisis. It was time the world danced to my tune.

"Then the AARP letter arrived. Suddenly I'm being shoveled into the ground. I went from a kid to a senior citizen without ever being an adult."

Paul's AARP letter is a classic. Just reading it will turn your hair gray. It begins: "You paid your dues by living through some of the most difficult and trying times in American History."

That solemn capitalized "American History" makes you feel like a museum piece already.

"You endured, you survived—one crisis after another. The effects of a devastating depression. The most destructive war the world has ever known."

If you turn fifty this year, you were born in 1939. You were barely a toddler when the depression was over. By the end of World War II you were only nine years old. You didn't have a date with American History. You were too young to go out. This letter must be for your parents.

But the AARP letter says, "We need you. You need us. Because AARP gives you and all people fifty and over a strong voice that government hears . . . That's how we make our views heard on programs and legislation that are vital to all of us. Social Security . . . Medicare . . . improved pension coverage . . . "

Social Security? Medicare? Isn't this invitation a little premature? You weren't planning to retire for fifteen years. It's like being invited to a sweet sixteen party when you're twelve months old. Paul's letter said AARP membership would also give him "practical solutions to many of your everyday problems."

Here's a problem AARP thought an active, attractive fifty-year-old would have: "As I grow older, I'm driving less, so I think my automobile insurance rates should be reviewed accordingly . . . "

Then they offered the poor old coot a group hospital plan and promised "no AARP member refused coverage." No matter what the state of his aging body.

Paul isn't the only fifty-year-old plagued by AARP letters. Even people who shrug them off may have to comfort devastated friends.

Sandy got stuck on AARP's mailing list for several years. She said, "They never let you forget you're getting older. Those letters started coming for me when I turned forty-eight. I never joined, but I got two a week. They say 'AARP' in big letters right on the envelope, so everyone can see it."

I called AARP headquarters in Washington. They said most letters to fifty-year-olds come from the insurance services department.

"We do our best to start sending letters at age fifty, or in the month just before," said an AARP spokeswoman. "The names come from list brokers, magazine subscriptions, departments of motor vehicle registration and other sources."

Do you get many complaints?

"No, not particularly," she said. "If someone wants their name taken off our mailing list, we will. I suppose there are people who are sensitive about age, but we certainly don't think it's 'devastating' to be fifty. Our organization represents people age fifty and older."

But isn't fifty too young for Medicare and retirement?

"Our name can be misleading," the spokeswoman said. "We also help people plan for retirement. Age fifty is not too soon to start making your retirement years better."

Fair enough. Even Paul understood.

"It's not a bad idea," he said. "But AARP emphasizes the wrong things. All that talk about Medicare, motel discounts and a free subscription to *Modern Maturity* magazine will turn you into a sedate old person.

"If AARP gave me something interesting, like a discount on Glenlivet scotch and a subscription to *Penthouse,* I'd join."

A little tactful packaging would help, too. AARP might reach more fifty-year-olds without embarrassment if they sent their letters in a plain brown wrapper. And marked them: "For Mature Adults Only."

66. *Ten Nights of Glory*

Last year, Joe Prichard was teaching sixth-graders in De Soto, Mo., and playing part-time in a couple of bands. He was forty, and he'd been doing the same thing for almost twenty years.

It was a pleasant life—a small-town school and some small-time bands:

a lot of weddings, some clubs, a little money.

"I like teaching," Joe said, "but I've always wondered just how well I could do if I spent more time with my music."

He doesn't wonder any more. Joe took a one-year sabbatical. He wound up playing for Chuck Berry for ten nights and twelve performances. He had limos in Atlantic City and stayed at Las Vegas casino hotels.

This was a long way from the sixth grade. "They sure treat you different when you're with Chuck Berry," Joe said.

It all started during a jam session at a St. Louis saloon called Spatz. "One thing I did during my time off was sit in with a lot of good local bands. One Saturday, I was jamming with Marcel Strong, and Chuck's daughter, Ingrid Berry, listened to me play. She came up and sang with us. Afterward, I talked with her. Ingrid and her husband, Chuck Clay, work together in music. I thought I'd ask about playing for them.

"But Ingrid said, 'We've been working with Dad.' I figured I couldn't beat that, so I didn't expect to hear from her again.

"Then one Wednesday she phoned and said Chuck Berry might need a piano player in Atlantic City. She called again on Friday and said they needed me that night. I flew to Philadelphia. A limo took me from Philly to Atlantic City. The traffic was so heavy, there wasn't time for a rehearsal. Before the show, all I had was a five-minute sound check. Chuck Berry showed me a few things, then told me to watch him."

Joe says he only read Chuck's signals wrong once. "I saw him pointing his guitar down. I thought he meant 'get down,' so I launched into a solo. What he really meant was turn the volume down. He laughed about it later.

"I wasn't nervous. It was complete and total pleasure.

"I was even mentioned in the newspaper review, sort of. It said Chuck's original pianist, Johnnie Johnson, 'wasn't at the piano; no explanation was offered and nobody at the showroom noticed.'

"If they didn't notice me, I figured I did OK.

"Then Chuck asked me for Las Vegas a couple of weeks later. I never thought I'd get to repeat the process. 'Process'—I'm talking like a teacher."

But he sure wasn't living like one. Once again, it was limos and the best hotels. "Chuck sure treats his band right.

"In Las Vegas, when we pulled up to the hotel, there was this big sign: 'Bally's Hotel Presents Chuck Berry and Jerry Lee Lewis.'

"I thought, 'Oh, no. I'm going to have to follow Jerry Lee Lewis on what's left of the piano after he plays it.' I was scared. But then I thought, 'I get to play the same piano as him. And I'm on the same stage as Chuck Berry. I'm with rock-and-roll history.' "

Joe said Berry's show includes his hits, like "Maybellene" and "Johnny

B. Goode."

"And when Chuck does blues numbers, the audience gets very quiet and respectful. They listen to the message. I've seen rock concerts where the audience is jumping up and down and partying. They're paying more attention to the party than what's on stage. But Chuck has a way of riveting their attention."

Joe sounds almost as starry-eyed as one of his sixth-graders. "No two shows are alike. That's what is so exciting. He's so inventive. When I'm on stage, I've always got this feeling he's going to do something he's never done before.

"Even if Chuck Berry never calls me again, I've had ten of the greatest nights of my life," Joe said. "Every time I heard him sing his song, 'Promised Land,' I thought, 'That's where I am.' "

67. Asking for the Moon

Wendy's 71-year-old grandma was in town recently for a visit. "Grandma loved St. Louis," Wendy said. "She had to see everything."

That ought to make the tourist people happy. But they may not like Granny's favorite sight.

Wendy said her grandmother enjoyed her visits to the Arch. The Zoo. Union Station. Shaw's Garden. But you know what Grandma liked best about St. Louis?

"She got mooned," Wendy said.

Mooning is a ritual in which a person—usually a gentleman—exposes his posterior. When a person goes mooning in a car with the windows rolled up, that's called a "pressed ham."

"Grandma lived most of her life in Alabama," Wendy said. "She's never been to the big city before. Being mooned was the most exciting thing that ever happened to her."

Here's how it happened. "My mom took Grandma to a Wayne Newton concert," Wendy said. Wayne Newton is disgustingly wholesome. Just the thing for your sweet old mother.

"But one of the guys in the band dropped his pants, and mooned the audience," Wendy said. "He was wearing red underwear. Grandma thought it was real funny."

Grandma was savvy enough to realize this was only a half-moon at best. But for a while it looked like she might see a full moon.

"The next night my mother took Grandma to a nice restaurant. This guy came up and knocked on the window. Grandma didn't pay much attention to him until the waitress said, 'The last time someone knocked on the window, he mooned the place.' "

Who was the moonie? A street person? A wino? Or some other low form of city life, like a yuppie?

"We're not sure," Wendy said. "It all happened so fast. But Grandma was so excited. She spent the rest of the meal waiting to get mooned."

Nothing happened. The mooner never dropped in. Or down. But that didn't mean Grandma's trip had a disappointing end.

"She could hardly wait to get home and tell everyone about her visit. It's given her a whole new view of St. Louis."

Maybe our city leaders will take another look, too. They work hard to hound souvenir sellers, jugglers and roving musicians off the streets. The few who are permitted are up to their rear ends in regulations.

And this isn't happening just in St. Louis. Cities all over the country, hoping that visitors will drop their dollars, are doing their best to remove the riff-raff.

But if Wendy's grandma is any indication, we need some unplanned excitement on the street. Some wicked-looking musicians. Slick street vendors. Maybe a few public-spirited citizens could volunteer to moon tourists. Anything to improve the city's image.

St. Louis is the rehab capital of the country. But you can make a place too nice and neat. Tourists don't come to a city just to look at the flower planters, cute street signs and old-fashioned street lights.

They want more than tidy little tourist areas. They can get that at a nice theme park. And Disney World does it much better.

People go to the city because they like a little sleaze. Not a lot. Just a few surprises. A hint of sin. Even respectable women of seventy-one. It wouldn't cost anything to ease up on the street ban. It's not like people are asking for the sun and the stars.

Just the moon.

68. Red Necks and White Collars

The public relations woman approached the subject delicately. Would I like to do a story about stress and the urban yuppie? These stressed-out yuppies "lived next door to people who have largely opposing values."

You mean rednecks?

"Uh, yes. Although that's not quite how I'd say it."

But not discussing a problem openly only makes it worse. Just think of those young urban professionals stuck next to those old urban problems.

Stop that snickering, you insensitive lout. I've discovered a brand-new social ill.

St. Louis is unusual, the PR woman said, because most yuppies here live with their own kind, usually in the suburbs. "But what about those 'urban yuppies' who live in the city?" These city neighborhoods often have rehab areas combined with unregenerate—even degenerate—

neighbors.

Kathy Y. Randall is assistant program director of Lutheran Medical Center's Psychiatric Institute on the city's South Side. She sees some of these distressed city yuppies and understands their problems.

"My boss and I both live in the city," Kathy said. "Stress is the yuppie disease. We were talking and I said, 'But what about us urban yuppies?' Not that I consider myself a yuppie."

None of us do.

"But in the yuppie areas of the county, you see your own kind at the supermarkets, bars, and restaurants. In the city, no two people are alike. Yuppies moved to the city because they want to mix with people who aren't clones of themselves."

Yup, life is a little harder when you send in the clones. "You can't go to my city supermarket for pate. You can't dash in for a few things at the beginning of the month. That's when the government checks come out and there are long lines."

And city yuppies can't flaunt the symbols of success. "You can't show off your new BMW, or it may get ripped off. In my neighborhood, a garage is a big status symbol. It means you can have the status car. It's also easier to make an impression in the city. A BMW is nothing in the county." It's so much easier to keep up with the city Joneses.

"My husband and I both like being close to our offices. In the city, I don't have the stress of driving in highway traffic. But I do have the stress of being too close to my office and running into my clients all the time. My husband runs into his clients, too. And he's a city prosecuting attorney.

"In fact, sometimes we share clients."

And it can be stressful to meet some of the people her husband knows. "Even when they're friendly. We were at neighborhood bar, and the bouncer shakes my husband's hand and says he did a good job prosecuting him for murder.

"It's difficult getting county people to visit our neighborhood. They ask dumb questions like, 'Can I bring my car? Do you carry a gun?' Some are afraid to sit outside in our yard. They have very unrealistic fears."

There are also realistic fears. "Fear of crime adds to yuppie stress, especially when you read about a serious crime two or three blocks from your house."

Even among city yuppies, there are many differences. Some are guppies (gay urban professionals) or buppies (black urban professionals).

Then there are those neighbors with "largely opposing values." The ones who wear tattoos instead of Polo shirts.

"One woman I know lived in a $100,000 city house," Kathy said. "The redneck next door blocked her driveway with junk cars. The son was drunk and fought with his parents on the front lawn. They were in some branch of law enforcement, so the family brandished weapons.''

The traditional advice to ''talk to your neighbor in an open and adult manner'' just doesn't work. ''They might put sugar in the gas tank. Set trash fires. Or worse.''

So how do you cope?

''By ignoring them as much as possible, until an opportunity comes along to turn them in. You might want to make friends with a nice police officer.''

You might also use the traditional city weapon, calling the city inspector. ''They may give your neighbor a ticket for their trash. That doesn't really do much, but it gives you a good feeling.''

Kathy says the redneck neighbor isn't really the cause of stress—just the trigger that sends the yuppie scurrying for help. ''Stress is usually some combination of work, personal relationships, and leftover childhood issues.

''If you live in the city, accept your neighbors. You don't have to marry them, or even party with them. Just live with them. If you really want homogeneous neighbors, move to the suburbs.''

Then you won't find situations like this: ''Once we were playing volleyball in the back yard. The homeless man who patrols our alley for aluminum cans yelled, 'Hurry up and drink your beer, we need the cans.'

''We said, 'They'll be out tomorrow.' Our suburban friends found that very upsetting.''

Some of those ''largely opposing values'' seem to be rubbing off on the yups. Kathy swears that she's seen yuppies digging in the trash bins behind an elegant city florist's shop.

''They were looking for slightly wilted flowers and old potpourri.''

69. Finally: A Lottery Winner Who Acts Like One

Christopher Keller of St. Louis is my hero, and not just because he won $4 million in the Illinois lottery.

It's because Chris acted like a winner.

On Saturday, Chris was an appliance salesman making $20,000 a year. On Sunday, when he got the news, he drank champagne. Planned a party for his 200 closest friends. And kissed his job goodbye.

''It's vacation time,'' he told the newspapers. ''I just don't want to sell appliances any more. Would you?''

No. But I've seen too many new millionaires who say, ''Well, I'm gonna pay all my bills and maybe go to Hawaii, but I'll keep my job at the rendering plant.''

You think I'm kidding? Look at this story about a Missouri man who'd just won $6 million in November. The winner "had no definite plans for spending the money and would probably continue working at his job at the lead smelting refinery," it said. "He has worked for the firm for twenty years.

" 'The first thing I'm going to do is consult our tax attorney,' he said."

It's enough to make you weep. And he's not the only one. Remember the Kansas City nurse who won $4.5 million last October?

"She said she planned no vacations and would keep her nursing position," the AP reported. "She said her immediate plans were to pay some bills and then talk to a financial adviser. 'It would be nice to be debt-free,' she said."

And she can probably manage it on $225,510 a year for twenty years. That's about what Christopher's going to get.

I think people who give interviews like this don't deserve the money. They have a duty to the rest of us wage-slaves who dream of winning the lottery and setting ourselves free.

I don't care if the nurse and the lead smelter chuck everything and run off to Tahiti later. The damage has been done. In the first rosy—or is it emerald—glow from those new millions, the winners can afford to throw caution to the winds.

But most of them don't. I checked the newspaper files for 1988 and 1987. The results were so depressing, I couldn't go on.

I saw stories about seventeen new lottery millionaires. Only a measly three winners said they would quit their jobs. Three said they didn't know. And eleven said they would keep on working.

These weren't people with cushy jobs. The chairman of the board rarely buys tickets. The winners included a bus driver, a bartender, and a hospital worker.

A school bus driver probably has the worst job in the world. How'd you like to be shut up in a yellow tin can with a bunch of loud kids? So when one bus driver won over $2.2 million in the Missouri Lotto game, you'd expect him to say adios, right?

Wrong. He said he'd keep his job.

Did you ever tend bar? It's no fun standing on your feet all day, waiting on drunks. So what happened when a bartender won $10 million in January? She said she'd keep on working because, "I'm too young to retire."

But first she'd have a wild fling, buying braces for her granddaughter, and sending her grandkids to college. She might also take a trip or two.

But the worst was the guy who waited until the next year to file his claim, so he could save on taxes. He lucked into $6.7 million, but he waited from Halloween to January so he could save a measly "several thousand dollars." It's scary.

I swear the article said he bought a house for his old mother in Peoria and a car for his father-in-law. And he's going to keep his job flakking for the Illinois governor.

Even when some lottery winners do quit, it hardly seems worth it. In 1985, a man won $7 million. He quit his job. But he didn't quit bargaining for everything, a recent story said.

"I'm 63 years old and I'm not going to change my habits," he said. His wife clips coupons and buys her clothes on sale. She also does her own housework and cooking.

I know that Chris will probably calm down in a couple of weeks, go to school and put his money away with barbed wire and snakes all over it so he can't spend it. At least, that's what his mother says.

But in the meantime, he's enjoying it. For all of us. I tried to talk with him, but his mom, JoRee Keller, said, "It's been a zoo here. Chris has gone away for a few days where he can recover." But he'll be back soon to pick up the partying.

"None of us had any money," she said. "I'd just bought a book store in University City called The Book Store. His brother Murray was getting married, but we couldn't afford anything but a quiet ceremony at my house.

"Now Chris is footing the bill for a big wedding. He even rented a stretch limo with a wet bar to take the wedding party to get their tuxes. I'm so glad he won. Now I won't have to get the house ready for all those people.

"He needed this break," she said. "He was driving this old Cougar, nursing it along. Two years ago, the power steering went out, and he's had to drive it without any ever since. We couldn't scrape together the $900 to get it fixed.

"Chris just paid the last payment on his auto loan in January. Saturday night, the miserable car died, right in front of the house, hissing and smoking. Sunday, Chris found out he won the lottery.

"After the dust settled, Chris went out on the front porch, shook his fist at the car and said, 'And you, sucker, are history.'

"Then he had it hauled away."

70. The Art of City Living

Marge finally admitted defeat and moved out of the city. She was driven out by her neighbors. They criticized her housekeeping. They complained about every weed in her yard. They said her window sills needed dusting.

And the neighbors were not perfect. Their relatives parked campers and trailers in front of Marge's house. Their errant pets fertilized her lawn.

"One day, my neighbor discussed how long she had lived in the neighborhood," Marge said. "She said she was so happy she would never move.

"That same evening I called a real estate agent and listed my house. I accepted the first offer and was gone within three weeks. I am now a happy resident of St. Louis county. My closest neighbor is half a mile away."

It's for the best, Marge. You don't have the right stuff to survive in the concrete jungle. My neighborhood, the South Side, would have had a great time with your neighbors. We can turn petty disagreements into major feuds.

The rich get lawyers, the poor get guns, but South Siders have more subtle weapons. They use the grudge, the glare, and the feud.

And St. Louisans have developed them into an art form. We never stoop to yelling. A good glare can stun someone into silence.

You can use the glare when a neighbor asks a nosy question or criticizes you.

"She said she heard the neighbors thought my lawn needed raking, but I just glared at her. She should look to the weeds in her yard," is typical South Side, and the first sign of trouble.

The glare has gone mobile. St. Louisans can glare going 70 MPH. When a driver cuts you off, you catch up with the creep, drive alongside, and glare. Honking and flipping the finger are for amateurs.

With time, you can cultivate your grievances into a real feud. Feuds are not undertaken lightly. They require wit and endurance.

A good feud will entertain you through the dull winters and long hot summers. It can involve everyone on the block. Soon you are all happily reporting each other to the city inspector, the health department, and the police.

Alas, some people are not worth feuding with. They do not have the skill or style to maintain this intimate relationship.

In that case, South Siders ignore them.

When South Siders discover they have been double-crossed by a neighbor or coworker, they wipe that person out of their life. They can look straight at the offenders, and not see them.

South Siders scorn the WASP habit of making social chitchat with enemies. That is unspeakably false. They also scorn the pop-psych advice to "discuss the problem in an open and adult manner."

They know some people are too twisted to change. Ignoring them is simple, clean, and convenient. The troublesome person ceases to exist in your world.

This leaves you more time to devote to feuds.

Family feuds are best. Then the relatives can choose sides and join in. The best family feud I know took place between a woman and her husband. For more than twenty years, they didn't speak to each other. If you went to their house, the woman would say, "Tell Harold dinner is on the table."

Harold would be sitting three feet from her, but he would turn to you and say, "Tell Mildred I'll be there in a minute, and I need a button sewn on my shirt."

During this time, the couple had two children. A wife has her duties, after all.

When Harold died, Mildred wailed, "I've lost the only man I ever loved."

It was worse than that. She now had no one NOT to talk to.

71. *Questions You Don't Ask Rehabbers*

Several years ago, I rehabbed an old house. Some of my relatives did not approve. They lived in the suburbs, where everything was new.

"It took us three generations to get out of the slums," said one, "and you've moved back in."

You either like old houses, or you don't. If you don't, then that carved woodwork is a dust catcher. The high ceilings waste heat. The red brick doesn't look mellow, just old and grimy.

We rehabbers know this. At night, when we turn off the lights and we can't see the antique stained glass, we worry about the antique plumbing. We envy new house owners their uncracked ceilings, garbage disposals and showers. We'd do anything to have them—except move into a new house.

But you don't have to rub it in.

Lee the Rehabber is working on his next renovation project. He'd like to rehab the attitudes of his suburban friends and relatives. Or at least get them to shut up.

"You won't believe what I have to listen to when they visit their city friend. That's me," Lee said. "We rehabbers could murder these insensitive hicks and get away with it, if we were truly tried by a jury of our peers.

"All they want are new malls, new houses, and new cars. They'd tear down the whole city and start over every twenty years. Even my own mother and grandmother belong to this group, but I won't murder them."

That's nice, Lee.

To make sure you don't get your jaw renovated on your next visit to a rehabber's home, take a look at Lee's list. This is one preservation project that may interest you.

15 Things You Never Say to a Rehabber

1. Why do you want to live here?

" 'Here' is the city, versus the suburbs or the country where they live," said Lee. This is always a disapproving question.

2. Why don't you drop the ceilings? You could save money on your heating bill.

"Yes, but then the air conditioning bills go up. Besides, eight-foot ceilings look funny with nine-foot windows."

3. Why don't you get wall-to-wall carpeting?

"They always ask this right after you've spent three weeks and $600 refinishing the floor," Lee said. "Or worse, you've paid someone $2,000 to do it."

4. Why don't you get rid of those old rugs and get wall-to-wall?

"This one really gets a rehabber going. The old rug is a ninety-year-old Oriental worth $6,000. Wall-to-wall only lasts five to ten years."

5. Why don't you get rid of that old light fixture and put in a ceiling fan or track lights?

"I have nothing against ceiling fans," Lee said. "But that 'old light' is a brass fixture from the turn of the century. I've just scraped ten coats of paint off it. And the cut-glass shade is worth more than most ceiling fans."

6. How can you stand that woodwork? Why don't you paint it white?

See No. 3.

7. Why don't you cover that old brick with insulated siding?

"Fists clench on this one," said Lee.

8. Why don't you remodel the bath and get a vanity and a new tub with a shower?

"I just did remodel the bath. I threw away the modern vanity and installed a pedestal sink and a claw-foot tub."

9. You know, you ought to concrete over that old brick patio. It would be easier to clean.

"The old brick patio is new. I just finished it."

10. How can you stand all this old furniture?

See No. 4.

11. Why don't you panel?

"$*/-!!"

12. My grandma had one of those and she threw it out.

"Yeah, so did my grandma," said Lee, "and she didn't know she threw

out $500, either.''
13. My grandmother had dishes like that and she got them for free.
''Antiques are funny, aren't they?''
14. You've lived here how long and this is all you've got done?
''Don't remind me.''
Lee added this last one to the list in mid-August:
15. How can you stand to live without central air?
''I can't!''

72. Snow Jobs

In winter, there's only one thing worse than being hit with a load of snow—being hit with a load of snow stories. I'm wading waist-deep through drifts of cute stories, with my heart warmed and my fancy tickled.

I've heard about the grandmother who skied five miles for milk and a magazine. The couple who held a barbecue in the snow. And the woman who was trapped in the house with fourteen seven-year-olds. Or was it seven fourteen-year-olds? It was too awful to read further.

Meanwhile, saints have stalked the streets, helping trapped motorists.

I've just one question: Where are all the creeps? It's time the selfish and venal did their duty. It's up to them to save us from all this goodness.

I'll go first. It took the heroic effort of three people to get me to work Monday morning. We dug out half an alley with a borrowed coal shovel.

We used a coal shovel because someone had stolen our snow shovel off the front porch. But none of us went to work because we were heroes.

I'd spent six hours Sunday playing Scrabble. After trying to make a word with four I's, a Q and a V, I'd rather dig out the alley. Two neighbors helped. One was a gentleman who had counted all the roses on his wallpaper. The other was a woman whose boss told her not to worry if her car wouldn't start: She could hitchhike into work. ''It's too awful for muggers and robbers to be out,'' the boss said cheerily.

The office cafeteria has had the Neil Simon special all week. It's something green—either very old meat or very new cheese. My friends are surly and tired of coping. We're even more tired of people bragging they're having fun. If you feel the same way, here are **Six Surly Snow Stories.**

1. The Dedicated Employee
Sunday, the Poplar Street bridge was blocked by wrecked and stalled cars. Yet at least one man made it across. A waiter at a downtown hotel literally ran to his job—a distance of twelve miles. Awesome! The man

only made the minimum wage.

Co-workers asked him why he did it.

"I had to," he said. "I drank my last can of Coors at 2 o'clock Sunday."

2. The Dedicated Doctor

"More snow," Lisa said despairingly, as she watched the white stuff swirling through the air. She looked out the window. She paced the floor. She called her psychiatrist.

"This snow is driving me crazy," she said. He sighed. "Do you know how often I've heard that today?"

3. The Fearless Driver

Saturday night, Dick was driving home in the ice and snow. Cars were skidding everywhere. "Don't be scared," Dick told himself. "They don't know how to drive. You'll be OK if you aren't scared."

Up ahead, Dick saw a tow truck. The big kind, that tows trucks. It skidded off the road.

"Be scared," Dick said.

4. Helping Hands

Don H. has nothing but praise for his fellow citizens. "People are magnificent. When a car gets stuck, someone always stops to help. The finest example was in my neighborhood.

"A car was stuck at the foot of a steep, curving hill," Don H. said. "Everyone came out to help. Shoppers rushed out of nearby stores. Strong women put on their coats and ran outside. Sick men got out of their beds. Little children left their warm TV sets.

"They pushed the man up the steep hill. They shoveled out a spot for him to park his car. They carried him to his door."

He was the neighborhood bartender, coming to open the only saloon in walking distance.

5. A Mother's Love

A St. Louis mother was on a Colorado ski vacation when the storm hit Saturday. It took her forty-four hours to get home to her two young sons. She traveled by plane, train, jeep, and, finally, by foot. But she made it to her little ones.

The four-year-old said the present she brought him was "crummy." The two-year-old screamed continually. The loving mother hired a baby sitter and went back to work.

6. The Free Ride

Jill, a handsome single woman, desperately needed a lift home. Nobody was going her way.

Finally, she called me with good news. "I found someone," she said. "He's handsome. He has blue eyes and curly hair. And chains."

Great, I said. With chains on his car, he can get down your street.

"Car?" Jill said. "Oh, he has snow tires on his car."

73. *Eleven Ways to Tell If You're a Grownup*

I love to read advice columnists, but the problems don't seem to have much to do with my life. I don't care which way the toilet paper hangs— an issue that absorbed Ann Landers for weeks.

But I finally saw an advice column question that hit home. A woman named Barbara asked: "How does somebody know when she is grown up?"

"I still feel like a kid," Barbara wrote, "but I am going to be forty next year . . . . There are many things about growing up that I don't want to face, but I'm afraid I don't have much choice."

The advice columnist told her, "There are several characteristics of being grownup: a sense of who you are and what values you ascribe to consistently. A marketable skill that allows you financial independence. A state of emotional well-being that permits you comfort with yourself. The ability to look at a situation and make reasonable judgments about long-term consequences concerning specific behaviors.

"Finally, being an adult means . . . realizing that the standards and expectations you set for yourself have an effect on others."

The advice columnist sounded just like your mother: Grow up, go to work, pay your bills.

By those standards, I flunked. So did all my friends. But I have my own criteria for adulthood. Here are my Eleven Signs You're a Grownup.

1. Police officers and baseball players are younger than you.

I'm horrified when sportswriters call ballplayers "old" at thirty-five. Why, they're barely in their prime.

2. Your kids are a problem—and so are your parents.

It isn't fair. At the same time your children enter their terrible teens, your parents start acting up. They're irresponsible. They stay out too late. They drive like maniacs.

Worse yet, they are your kids' best friends, loaning them money and covering up for them. Pest calls to pest across the generations.

3. You read your first obituary with pleasure.

We finally got 'em.

4. You ogle someone cute and discover it's your friend's kid.

Eeek! The handsome young man in the skin-tight bicycle pants turns out to be your friend's son. The little kid you took to the zoo years ago. Auntie Elaine is a dirty old lady.

5. The music you like is on the oldies stations.

6. The clothes you wore in college are collectibles.

I overheard this depressing conversation between two young persons:
Girl 1: "Great peace sign."
Girl 2: "Thanks. It's an antique. It's my mom's."

That's when I remembered all those smart remarks I made about the funny-looking forties clothes on the late-night movies. God punished me.

7. You don't know the person on the cover of *People* magazine.

Even worse, you don't know who's on the cover of *Rolling Stone*. And if you do, you haven't heard their music.

8. You no longer know the new cars.

You can't even tell this year's Mustangs, Corvettes, and T-Birds. When you buy a car, you want to know things like miles per gallon, trade-in value, and is there room for the kid's hockey sticks.

9. Nothing's been any fun since the sixties.

You thought when Nixon resigned it was the beginning. Actually, it was the end.

10. You catch yourself saying, "That was twenty years ago . . ."

Just like an old duffer. Worse yet, you were an adult twenty years ago.

11. You've outlived at least one doctor.

They're looking young these days, too. I went along to the doctor's office with a friend. He wanted to talk to the doctor about his ninety-year-old mother's illness. The doctor seemed competent, even if he did have peach fuzz.

When we left the office, my friend said, "Are you sure he's old enough to be a doctor?"

"We can't get one her age," I said. "She's outlived everybody."

74. The Exotic Rituals of a St. Louis Summer

Have you seen those vacation commercials? I don't want to hurt any feelings, but the only way I'd spend thirty days in some of those eyesores is if I was sentenced by a judge.

But you wouldn't know it from the ads. They call these godforsaken holes "exciting." They talk about the "native traditions" and "colorful customs."

Those aren't colorful customs. Those are people doing the same thing, over and over. We've got plenty like them at home.

Lee the Rehabber thinks we could promote St. Louis with the same kind of vacation ads. I think he's right. Especially in my neighborhood, the South Side. Let's take a look at some of the colorful city customs we could feature.

1. Sacrificing a Live Child

This activity marks the official start of summer Saturdays. A live kid is sacrificed to appease father's wrath.

Saturday is chore day for dad, and he will spend these first fine days of summer cleaning the basement and the garage. Soon the whole neighborhood sounds with his fatherly cries: "Who left my hammer outside in the grass? It's rusty!" "Where's my Phillips screwdriver?"

The smart kids disappear out the door. The dumb ones escape upstairs to their rooms, where they are flushed out by their mother. "It's too nice to be inside hanging around the house," Mom says. "It's much healthier outside."

Not with father looking for the kid who ruined his hammer. The child is caught, and sentenced to pull weeds for the rest of the day. His Saturday is dead.

This Sacrifice of the Live Child appeases father's wrath. He calms down, and begins putting up the screen doors. The kid pulls a bucket or two of weeds, then slowly works his way to the edge of the lawn and freedom.

2. Ritual Walk-Sweeping

The women of the neighborhood sweep the sidewalks daily. This ritual sweep is a symbol of the neighborhood's cleanliness, inside and out.

It's also the best way to check out what's happening: How long has the handsome electrician been at the redhead's house? What did the department store truck deliver to your neighbor's?

This valuable information is transmitted over the back fence Monday morning during another neighborhood ritual:

3. The Ceremony of the Three Sheets to the Wind

On Mondays, the laundry is hung outside on clothes lines, while the women make this ritual chant, "I think sheets smell so much better when you hang them outside."

This ceremony takes a lot of paraphernalia. There are the clothes poles. And clothes props. And the bag filled with clothes pins.

4. Native Markets

Also known as estate sales or yard sales. These are great places to pick up souvenirs of your visit to this exciting place.

Look for good buys on small colorful handmade goods, such as knitted toilet paper covers in the shape of top hats. You can also buy old furniture, broken toasters, and children's clothes, size 6X.

To find a sale, look for the handmade signs stuck on telephone poles and sycamore trees.

Estate sales are very emotional. This is the first time the family of the deceased will see their aunt's sofa without slip covers.

Here's how to tell a good yard sale: There will be a stationary bicycle, bought when the sale giver went on a diet in 1976.

5. Native Games

St. Louisans like to drink beer. Thanks to the German influence, they can't bear to waste anything. Not even the bottle caps.

That's why you'll find games using broomstick bats and bottlecap "balls" springing up in the alley behind the corner bar. The more affluent play cork ball.

Both the cork ball and the bottle caps can break windows. This helps
the neighborhood indulge in another favorite sport—feuding.

6. Stoop-Sitting

Some native peoples parade around the town square. In my
neighborhood, they sit on the stoop and sip beer. Good, cold, American
beer.

Diet soda is not permitted.

7. Ted Drewes Hanging Out

I know the guide books recommend going to Ted Drewes Frozen
Custard on Sundays.

But insiders know Ted's is a little touristy on weekends. They go to
Ted's weekdays only, and they prefer the store on South Grand. Real
South Siders also eat ice cream at Bailey Farm Dairy. And I'm not giving
you the address.

8. Belly-Bombing and Big-Gulping

Big Gulps are those huge cheap sodas from 7-Eleven. This is a summer activity. Big Gulps cause frostbite in the winter.

Belly Bombers are White Castles. They taste best after midnight and
before you turn thirty.

75. Some Day Bosses May Butter Up Employees

I've made my last nasty joke about California. You won't hear me
saying California has more fruitcakes than a Christmas bake sale. Not
any more. I have maligned that fine state.

I never realized what a workers' paradise it is. In California, you can
get workers' compensation for stress.

That's right. If you work for a jerk, you can hit the company for a
mental stress claim.

Since everything from alfalfa sprouts to highway snipers starts in
California and heads east, some day you could be collecting against the
supervisor who yelled at you.

Right now, it's possible to file a mental stress claim in Missouri—but
you probably won't collect. At this time, our state has no reported stress
cases, and no known awards. That's because Missouri won't take just
a doctor's report. They make you prove it by the rules of evidence.

Most of us have had rotten bosses. Not to mention mean, crazy bosses.
We either put up with them or start looking for another job.

I went to work at sixteen. In the last twenty years, I've worked for
a lot of bosses. Some were very good. Some were incredibly bad.

I've had bosses who used drugs at the office. Bosses who sold drugs at
the office. Bosses who lied. Hung out in restroom stalls and reported

employee gripes to management.

I've worked for female bosses who favored their boyfriends. Male bosses who promoted their tootsies. Some of these bosses were headaches and industrial-strength pains in the neck. But they probably weren't any worse than the ones you work for.

And what really drives you nuts is that there's no hope. You can't do anything to get rid of your bad boss.

But under the California system, you could file a claim based on that distressing fact. In fact, you can claim just about anything causes you stress.

"All it takes is a doctor to say the stress was work-related," said Don Petersen. Just saying his title must be stressful. Petersen is chief of the information and assistance bureau, division of industrial accidents, for the state of California.

"We've had workers say they suffered from stress because their bosses yelled at them," Petersen said. "Or they had to work against deadlines. Or they worked for a convenience store and were afraid they'd be held up."

And then what happened?

"You can be paid up to $224 a week for a temporary disability during the healing period, plus medical benefits. If your doctor says you have a permanent disability, you would receive an additional award."

Petersen gave an example any worker could identify with. "We have a lot of prison guards who file stress claims. Because of riots and other problems at work, their jobs become too stressful. A guard with a twenty percent permanent disability would get an award of about $10,000, plus help in training for a new job. And, if the doctor says it's necessary, the guard would receive additional medical care."

This gets a company right where it hurts. In the wallet. A boss who triggers too many stress claims could become a liability. It might be cheaper for the company to remove the bad boss. Except then, under California civil law, the boss could turn around and sue the company for wrongful discharge. And juries are very kind. One California law firm says the average award for wrongful discharge is about $424,500.

Your bad boss could wind up rich. The thought is so distressing, you might have to file another claim.

The whole system is causing chaos in California. In six years mental stress claims have increased an amazing 531 percent.

"It's just killing employers," Petersen said. "The costs are running up fast. There are attempts to limit stress claims with legislation, but so far without success."

Naturally, by the time Missourians start collecting for stress, we'd expect the bugs to be out. We'd also expect stress claims to change office life as we know it.

Instead of buttering up your bosses, telling them their proposals were brilliant, and asking if they've lost weight, your boss would be worried about you. Are you happy? Content? In a good mood?

Not feeling, er, stressed, are we?

The office atmosphere would be more polite, quiet and courteous. You'd rarely hear any ugly four-letter words.

Like "work."

76. The Two-Door Status Symbol

You know the worst part about the new garage? It was my idea.

The garage is the ultimate city status symbol. In rehabbed neighborhoods, nobody's impressed by stained glass and mahogany. We all have that. Garages are the real prizes. They protect your car from the local light-fingered lads. That way you can have another city status symbol—a car with a radio.

Like most rehabbers, we bought our city house cheap back in the seventies. So it was a real shock to find out what a new garage cost.

"We got a great estimate," said Don H. He was actually smiling when he said, "It's $10,000."

Is Michelangelo painting the ceiling? I thought we were getting a garage, not the Sistine Chapel.

"Where have you been?" asked Don H. "That's a good price for a three-car garage. You know what things cost now?"

I felt like those old women who tip the handyman ten cents. And before you get too impressed by the three cars, we have a two-family flat.

Michelangelo didn't paint the garage, but it was still a masterpiece. It had all the things city people covet: new plumbing, new gutters, new siding, and a roof that didn't leak. In fact, if we could have found a way to get our cars into our second-floor flat, we would have moved into the garage and parked in the house.

Finally, it was finished. The garage would have two doors for three cars. One door was big enough for two cars. Don H. and the folks downstairs would park there.

"You get your own space," said Don H., sounding like someone from California. He meant I would park in the one-car section. He proudly handed me the automatic garage-door opener and held open my car door. We drove around to the alley for the garage grand opening.

As we approached, I pressed the door opener. It glowed like a single red, hungover eye. The door rumbled open. The garage space shrank. It didn't look big enough for a bicycle rack. The front end of my car grew three feet, until it seemed longer than a stretch limo. And much wider. How was I going to get this car into that little space?

Well, I couldn't leave it in the alley all night. I backed up to take aim and saw the city dumpster was taking up most of the alley. Worse yet, the dumpster had big, clawlike things reaching out to scratch my car. There was no room to maneuver.

That's when I remembered I'd never parked in a garage before.

Well, there's always a first time. I swung it in, and wiped out the right side of the car. Along with a good chunk of the garage.

I couldn't believe it. I'd wrecked my car. Just like a cartoon wife. I'd just set the women's movement back fifty years. Not to mention the damage to my bank account.

You had to appreciate the irony. The car didn't have a scratch on it, until I hit the garage that was supposed to protect it.

Naturally, it wasn't my fault. The garage was too small. And the dumpster was in the way. That's why I couldn't get in there.

For a month, I drove the banged-up car, while I gritted my teeth and tried to get into the garage. I remembered all the times I'd waited impatiently in the alley while the old duffers slowly opened their garage, inched the car in, then backed it in and out several times. Now I knew why they went so slow.

To make it worse, Don H. was having no trouble at all. His car slid in like it was greased. It was also slightly smaller than mine. It would fit easier on the one-car side.

Don H. agreed to make the switch. As soon as my car got back from the body shop, we would swap garage spaces.

And so we did. I picked up my shiny, newly repainted car from the shop. He parked his car in my old spot. It went right in, without any problem.

Then I swung into the new garage, and wiped out the other side of my car.

77. Guide for a Summer Gala

The summer party season is heating up. But fashionable hostesses always look so cool on the night of their gala. How do they do it? What is their secret?

Beats me. I don't know any of those people.

But I do know four successful South Side hostesses. And they'll spill the secrets of a good summer party. Let me introduce Joann Brueckner, Kathy Moore, Betty Mitchell and Barb Hartman. This is their

Guide for a South Side Summer Gala

"The proper place to have a get-together is in your back yard," Kathy said. For a good time, "remember to use the pooper-scooper."

"Before the party, walk the neighborhood and collect all the coolers and grills you need. And remember to invite all the neighbors so they won't call the police when your party gets noisy."

Food: "South Siders believe in two entrees: pork steaks and chicken," Joann said.

Of course, you'll have a catered affair. "Call everyone and have them bring a covered dish," she said. "A summer party should have two kinds of potato salad, German and mayonnaise. Three bean salad, made with bottled Italian dressing. Deviled eggs. Macaroni—not pasta—salad."

Don't forget the "doctored" baked beans. That's canned beans improved with some of the following: French's mustard, ketchup, Karo syrup and onion flakes.

Some health nuts put out a tray of vegetables. Fortunately, there's always a fattening dip.

"Dessert is German chocolate cake and Popsicles. Or you can send out," Kathy said. "You send out the wives to Ted Drewes for frozen custard."

The right food tastes best on the right china. "You must use full-size Chinette plates."

Booze: "The proper wine is Walgreens special on white zinfandel. Anheuser-Busch products are served exclusively. Otherwise it's BYOB."

Lighting: Pretty but practical. Our hostesses use citronella candles and fruit lights strung across the yard.

Seating: Not enough folding chairs? It's socially correct to sit on the zoysia grass but not the lawn ornaments. Sitting on the concrete Virgin Mary is sacrilegious.

Dress: South Siders do not care to publicize designers' names. "Name brands are taboo except for Levi's," Kathy said. "Polyester is always proper. So are thongs."

Entertainment: Cork ball in the alley. Yard darts on the side lawn. Yelling at the kids to go next door to the sitter. And good music. That's any fifties rock-and-roll, especially the King.

Good Clean Fun: "The house must be cleaned top to bottom, even though your guests will never sit in a room," Joann said. "Make sure the scatter rugs and plastic runners are in place from the back door to the bathroom."

If it rains on gala day, a hostess must act fast. "Open the garage, move the car, and bring the barbecue grill in there," Kathy said.

"You certainly can't have all those wet, dirty people in your clean house."

78. Mastering the Fear of 40

It was 2:30 in the morning and Gayle Gibson was having nightmares. The big Four Oh was staring her in the face.

"I turn forty on July 22," she said. "I never kept track of my age before. I zipped through life just being me. I don't measure people in years. I know too many who transcend all age groups.

"Being thirty didn't faze me. But forty is another story. Suddenly I feel old and out of it, like I should trade in my cutoffs and start baking cookies. I even bought a muumuu to wear around the house. My neighbor laughed at me and said I still looked the same. But I don't feel the same."

Gayle finally mastered her fear of forty. She wrote me this letter explaining how.

"I don't know why forty bothers me," she said. "I don't see any lines on my face. Well, maybe a few, but I've always had those. At least I think I have. Unless my memory is going, too."

She did notice some signs of age. "Grocery baggers who used to flirt with me now call me ma'am and offer to help me with my bags.

"It seems like yesterday I was twenty. Then overnight I turned forty. Where did those years go? Maybe they went the same place socks go when you put them in the dryer.

"One day I was sitting on my parents' porch, thinking about turning forty, when I started sobbing uncontrollably. My dad tried to console me. He said, 'Big deal. Yesterday the war ended and I was coming home. That was forty-three years ago. And I'll tell you, kid, the older you get, the faster time flies.' "

Somehow, this didn't make Gayle feel better. Her mom didn't help, either. "She always said kids age you. I didn't know what she meant until recently. I started lying about my age. I told people I was thirty-two. Then some math whiz asked me why my son was twenty-one. I said I started young. I'd rather be a third-grade tramp than forty."

Flirting with younger men didn't help, either. "One day I was sitting by the pool when a good-looking hunk asked if he could lounge next to me. The hunk said he preferred 'older' women because they're smarter. He was amazed at my knowledge. I'd studied things like Sputnik and the Kennedys.

"Studied? All I did was turn on the TV.

"The Russians have a cure for the depression that accompanies aging. It's called vodka. You still age, but you don't care any more."

But before Gayle began working on her liquid assets she found a better solution.

"It's changed my life and my attitude," she said.

Gayle's solution didn't cost any money. She didn't need any dull seminars, diets, or exercise programs. She not only learned to live with being forty years old—Gayle went beyond it.

Here's what she did: "I tell everyone I'm forty-nine.

"They can't believe it. They say I look fantastic. They say I am remarkably young. They want to know how I have such a great body."

Instead of moping around in front of a mirror, looking for new lines and wrinkles, "I spend the day soaking up compliments. I feel good. I didn't like turning forty, but it's great being forty-nine.

"And when people say, 'Wow! You can't be forty-nine. You look at least ten years younger!' I always agree with them."

79. South Siders Have All the Right Moves

I am a third-generation South Sider, but I've abandoned some of the old neighborhood ways.

South Siders are supposed to be scrubby Dutch, but I'm not a fanatic cleaner like my grandmother. Every week, she took down her kitchen curtains, starched and ironed them. Mine have been up so long, you can boil them for soup.

Grandma used to boast her kitchen floor was so clean you could eat off it. You can eat off mine, too. I think there are enough crumbs down there for a meal.

But one thing hasn't changed. I still have that early spring itch.

In those gray, restless days before spring moves in, For Rent and For Sale signs pop up on South Side lawns like dandelions. We get the urge to pick up and move. Not too far, mind you. Not to another city, or even another neighborhood. We jump to another house, like fleas hopping around on the same dog.

One slow, dreary Sunday, I drove past a house for sale on my street. It was a big, red-brick pile, like every other house on the block. I knew—the hard way—that sturdy exterior probably concealed quirky wiring, a leaky roof, and uncertain plumbing.

Suddenly I wanted to buy it and move in. It's crazy, I know. But it's some warped instinct. In spring, some birds molt and some snakes shed their skins, but South Siders look for new places to move.

My South Side source, Janet Smith, gave a moving explanation for this phenomenon.

"If you move before the spring rains start, you can sell your house before the roof starts leaking," she said.

"And the weather is ideal for selling a house. Prospective buyers ask touchy questions like, 'Does the furnace work?' "

In the dead of winter, the correct answer is, "Sort of." But turn it on now and it feels like, well, a furnace blast.

"Turn on the air conditioner when it's ninety, and all you'll feel is lukewarm air. In chilly March, that same air feels frigid.

"If you have children, you have to pack up all the winter stuff anyway, and then unpack the spring clothes," Janet said. "That's so much trouble, you might as well move the whole house while you're at it.

"The kids will only be in school for one month. If you move, you'll only have to run them back and forth to their old school for a few weeks. If you can bully them into going to a new school, even better. They'll start making new friends, so they'll have kids to play with this summer.

"Your kids already know all they're going to know at school, so you can butter up the new teacher by telling her how you pulled your children out of the old place because you've heard such good things about her school.

"She knows they're probably trouble, but she won't care. She's only going to have them for a few weeks. Next year, they're some other teacher's problem."

Janet admits she, too, has the itch. "Everything looks gray this time of year," she said. "The days, the walls, the weather. That's when you get it."

Why don't we just take a vacation, and go some place warm for a week?

"Who can afford a vacation?" she said. "Even if we can, we can't justify such an indulgence. But a house is practical.

"I can't stand my living-room wallpaper. I never noticed it all winter, but now that there's more light, I can see it—and the cracks underneath. If we put up new paper, we'll have to take off five old layers. My husband knows this will be a major project. So he's nervous. All the South Side husbands are. If we don't move, it's time to drag out the ladders, paint and fix up."

For some men, moving may be easier. It's certainly more fun. They just borrow a friend's truck, down a few beers and sprain their backs carrying the china cabinet upstairs. Then they're absolved from all handyman chores till mid-summer.

And if you rent, moving to another apartment may be the only way to get the walls repainted. It's the one promise a new landlord keeps.

The search for a new place isn't easy, Janet said. "We're looking for something bigger and better with fewer steps to scrub—in an area where all the houses are basically alike. So we'll move into another house before the ceiling falls, the roof leaks, the furnace goes out and the air conditioner dies.

"And next year, when spring comes around, we'll get itchy."

80. How to Find a Classic City House

Fifteen years ago, it was easy to find a classic city house to rehab. A big, roomy brick house cost less than your car. To buy, that is, not to maintain.

Something is always going wrong with an old house. It has so many antiques: antique stained glass, antique fireplaces, and antique plaster, plumbing and wiring.

The only reason we can afford to live in an old classic is handymen like Lee the Rehabber—professional putterers who know how to patch plaster, sand floors, unstick windows, and gently stick you for money without bleeding you dry.

"I talk all my friends into buying classics," Lee said. "That's how I make my living. I'm never out of work."

So when a friend told Lee he wanted to buy a city house or flat to fix up, "I said to look for an old classic. These houses are very reasonable, very solid, and need no exterior improvements. And since the inside hadn't been 'remuddled,' they are cheap to gut and redo. He asked me to write out a list so when he found a classic he would know it."

Here is Lee's list.

21 Signs of a Classic City House

1. Classics should be bought from the owner. Cash sales are preferred. Look for the crucifix over the bed. The owner is probably a Catholic, a widow, and moving to her sister's or daughter's in the suburbs.

2. The house has all the original woodwork, never painted. Graining, an old-fashioned technique of painting woodwork golden-yellow so it looks like wood grain, is also fine.

3. Classics have footed bathtubs.

4. And space heaters. One in the kitchen, one in the dining room (also known as the master bedroom). No smart landlord puts too many improvements in a flat. Radiators are too new for most classic flats, though you may find them in single-family houses.

5. No cabinets in the kitchen, just a sink in one corner. A red-marble drain tray is a plus.

6. The kitchen has a large pantry. It should smell good.

7. The kitchen is the biggest room in the flat. There should be at least two layers of linoleum on the floor.

8. Other floors should be dark varnish or grained. Don't be surprised if you lift the area rug and find the floor underneath is unfinished.

9. None of the fireplaces work, but one mantel is fantastic. The fireplace grates may be covered with aluminum foil to keep out the cold air.

10. The ceilings have never been dropped.

11. A classic is brick with a flat roof.

This is a controversial opinion. Some say the more expensive peaked roofs last longer. But flat-roofers claim any leak can be fixed cheap with two gallons of tar.

12. Triple-track storm windows are the only energy-saving things on the whole building.

13. The front door is grained.

14. The gutters and trim are painted cream and green or white and green. The back porch is battleship gray.

15. The front steps are still the original stone, scrubbed white with Old Dutch cleanser every Thursday.

16. There's an old ash pit in the back yard. It can be concreted over, used to store old flower pots or grow sunflowers. Just so it has no ashes in it.

17. The lawn is zoysia. There's a rose garden in the back yard.

18. The garage is too small for anything but a compact car.

19. The house must be within walking distance of a good corner bar where the owner's husband hung out.

20. There's a small workshop in the basement where he liked to putter.

21. One final classic test. Step outside and take a deep breath. You should smell a brewery or a bakery. Unless you get the chemical plant first.

81. Soulard's Splendid Patina of Dirt

"I like Mayor Schoemehl," said South Side Rich. "He's done a great job planting flowers along the highway. But now I've got a piece of advice for Vince: Keep your bloomin' hands off Soulard Market."

But that's what the mayor wants to do—get the city out of running the 200-year-old farmers market. Under the new budget, the city would have a management firm run Soulard.

"That's wrong," Rich said. "The city should keep on running Soulard. Only the city government can keep it going the same gloriously inefficient way. A management firm is a mistake. They'll make it cost effective. They'll clean it up, raise the rents and chase off all the old cigar chompers who sell a couple of pounds of bananas.

"Before you know it, they'll be painting the place decorator colors like mauve and gray and putting out little tables with Cinzano umbrellas."

But the mayor's press secretary, Ed Bushmeyer, says that's not going to happen. "We want to contract out for the management," Bushmeyer said. "We will do nothing to disturb Soulard's unique flavor. But we do feel there's room for improvement. It needs some paint and sprucing up."

"Why can't the city handle this?" Rich said. "For a little paint, we don't need Michelangelo. We need Brod-Dugan.

"We should be careful what we clean. Soulard's splendid patina of dirt should not be disturbed. And if they fix up the restrooms, I'll never get in. They're crowded enough now, when only desperate people use them.

"If the city wants to clean something, they should clean out the parking meters around Soulard Market. That would really boost business.

"Soulard is the last bastion of capitalism," Rich said. "Some of those old bastions sell there every week, rain or shine.

"It's the best way for a city kid to get an education. Where else can you see over 200 entrepreneurs, all ready to cut one another's throats for a nickel?"

Soulard is where you learn there are honest business people, who will sell you a pound of produce for a fair price. There are generous people, who will throw in a little extra. And there are crooks, who will pack the bottom of the bag with mushy strawberries, and put a few pretty ones on top.

"It's part of your education to learn the market," Rich said. "It teaches you the first consumer law: Let the buyer beware."

I like to watch the regular Saturday drama of Papa. He's an old produce seller who, if he thinks you look green enough, will "miscount" your change—unless his daughters catch him. "Now, Papa," they will say, "you didn't count that right."

Somehow, the old pirate has produced an endless supply of honest daughters.

You also learn about your own greed. "Late on Saturday afternoon, it's bargain city at Soulard," Rich said. "That's where you can get things like sixty pounds of over-ripe bananas for a dollar. And learn thirty-seven banana bread recipes, to use up your bargain. That teaches you another important capitalist lesson—overproduction.

"Amazing feats are performed there," Rich said. "Soulard actually sells zucchini in the summer, when people can't give it away.

"At Soulard, you can identify the vegetable outside its natural habitat, the can.

"You can buy motor oil, whole jogging suits for $10, live plants. And duck eggs, for the world's largest fried eggs. Except when they have goose eggs.

"It's the only place I know where you can pick out your own live chicken. That's a lot more exciting than choosing your own lobster. You learn about wild life, too. They sell skinned rabbits, raccoons and possums."

Soulard is where I learned the proper way to sell a possum. When

I was about seven, I saw a skinned one, red and ugly, hanging up at a Soulard stall. I asked an old man what that was.

"Possum," he said. "Some people like to eat them."

How come they still have the feet and tails on?

"So you can tell them from rats," he said.

Editor's note: More than 10,000 people signed a petition to save Soulard Market. The mayor dropped his proposal. For now.

82. Don't Call Us

It finally happened. At least one federal agency has figured out how to isolate itself almost completely from your annoying phone calls.

They did it thanks to the telephone answering machine.

If you call most offices of the federal Immigration and Naturalization Service, you have to listen to a tape. The tape for the St. Louis INS office is nine minutes and twenty-seven seconds long.

Your tax dollar buys you the right to talk to a human being only between 2 and 4 P.M.

So what? You're no immigrant. Why should you worry about talking to anyone at INS?

Because every time you get a new job, you have to fill out an INS form. That's the law for every person in America, whether you're an immigrant or not. It's called Employment Eligibility Verification, but it's better known as Form I-9.

If you have a question about I-9, and you call the local INS office, you'll have to listen to that tape for a mind-numbing nine minutes and twenty-seven seconds.

I know. I timed it with a stop watch.

You have no choice. The only INS number listed in the phone book is the tape: 425-4532.

The message starts with a man saying you are calling an extension of the Ask Immigration system.

"If you need to hear this message in Spanish, please hold the (mumble) button until the message stops and then dial 019 on your phone," the tape said. "Otherwise, please remain on the line and this message will continue in English."

It doesn't. Next, you hear a Spanish-speaking woman. My section of the city has many Oriental immigrants. I'm sure they appreciate the Spanish parts.

Finally, the English-speaking man comes back on, talking about such subjects as the "Cuban-Haitian adjustment program," and the Immigration Reform and Control Act of 1986, and spewing out toll-free numbers.

Then we switch to the Spanish woman again.

After a while, the man starts talking English. Actually, it isn't quite English. It's a Washington dialect spoken only by bureaucrats. Here's a sample:

"In order to access any of the immigration information messages on this system, you must have a touch-tone phone. If you have called from a rotary home dial phone, although you cannot access any of the subject messages, you should remain on the line as your question may be answered by this general message."

Then again, it may not. But what's nine minutes to a taxpayer? A little later, the tape says:

"If you wish to provide information regarding a violation of the immigration law or if you wish to speak with a (mumble) officer, please call during office hours, Monday through Friday, excluding holidays, from 2 P.M. until 4 P.M."

Nice office hours. Don't you wish you could keep callers off your office phone except for two hours a day? If you can't call INS, they want you to write a letter or come see them.

The tape also says:

"If you are requesting status on an application, we are unable to provide you with such information over the telephone. It takes considerable time on the part of an officer to look for a file and therefore delays application processing."

Why? The officer can't be busy answering the phone.

But you can't stop the tape and ask it. You can't interrupt it. Sometimes, you can't even understand it.

The tape rolls on, talking about passports, fees, and how to "obtain a complete address for the INS Northern Regional Service Center."

It also gives you another number for more taped messages. Then it winds up with a questionnaire. Even on a recorded tape, the feds can't resist asking you to fill out more forms.

When I finally reached the St. Louis INS office, the real live person who answered the phone sounded almost as weary as the taxpayers who listen to the tape.

And with good reason. Now she answers INS questions and listens to complaints about the babbling tape.

"Washington D.C. in their infinite wisdom started it here about six weeks ago," the INS person said. "We're supposed to be cutting it down. But nobody's going to be happy with a tape. They want to yell at a real person.

"Until the tape, we answered the phone from 8 to 4:30. The main change now is more people come to the office."

No wonder. It takes less time to drive downtown than it does to listen to the recording.

But this was Washington's idea. I called the central INS office there for more information. The line was busy. Finally, on the fifth try, the phone was answered.

By a recording. A very long recording. But it promised if I hung on, a live person would answer my call in the order received.

So I hung on, while the tape played over and over. The taped voice droned on, telling me about federal forms and phone numbers. But I knew if I persevered, I would hear a human voice.

Then the tape stopped. This was it. I was going to talk to a live person.

Except the phone disconnected me. After thirty-one minutes of waiting.

INS has the perfect federal answering system. It leaves you so frustrated, you won't dare call and bother them.

It's the bright idea of Commissioner Alan C. Nelson. If you're tired of not being able to reach a human being at INS, I found out his Washington office number. It's (202) 633-1900.

Call him up.

And tell him to stick it in his ear.

Editor's note: At presstime, the nine minute and twenty-seven second INS tape had been cut to a measly five minutes. And Alan Nelson was no longer commissioner.

83. *Off the Wall at Blueberry Hill*

"Two wrongs won't make a right, but three rights will make a left."

"The less you bet, the more you lose when you win."

"If God had meant for us to walk around naked, we would have been born that way."

Call it off-the-wall humor. Or the ultimate combination of wit and style. Joe Edwards took the best graffiti from his saloon bathrooms and put them on a T-shirt. Now you can pay $10.50 for free expression. That's what a graffiti T-shirt costs at Blueberry Hill.

"I've always been thrilled with the bathroom graffiti here," Joe said. "The political graffiti during the Watergate years has never been surpassed. After that, I like the stuff from the last five years.

"I could kick myself, but I didn't start writing it down until the late '70s. Then one day it hit me. I could do something with this off-the-wall humor. I could put it on a T-shirt."

A white cotton Fruit of the Loom with scrawls like this: "Superman gets into Clark Kent's pants every morning."

Joe orders them by the gross, naturally.

He is amazed by how many people want to wear his graffiti shirts. "They want them so bad when I run out of the correct size, they'll buy one that doesn't fit properly. No other T-shirt has gotten this reaction."

Is the country going down the toilet? Or do they find meaning in messages like this: "If God had wanted us in the army, he would have given us green baggy skin."

Joe says he finds very few phone numbers and "John loves Suzy" on his walls. He credits his high-quality graffiti to his location. "Being in University City makes all the difference. Everyone here has something to say—and they do.

"It's interesting to read the graffiti and try to guess which ones came from the men's or the women's rooms. Sometimes they're in both. One side will hear about a good one and add it to their wall."

Joe was surprised to find "My mother made me a homosexual. *If I give her some yarn, will she make me one, too?*" in the women's room first. The men added it later.

"There are definite differences between men and women," he said. "Women are better at sexual innuendo. Politics is better in the men's. Philosophy is pretty equal."

Joe likes the philosophy of: "The tire is always flat on the bottom."

"Maybe I'm reading too much into it, but it seems to say something about society. It's always bad at the bottom.

"My favorite depends on my mood. Right now I like: 'The world is flat—Class of 1491.'

"And an old one: 'I'd rather have a free bottle in front of me than a prefrontal lobotomy.' "

Is that because you're in the bar business?

"No, I just like the way it rolls off your tongue."

"Nietzche is Pietzche" has a certain beat to it. And you could spend a lot of time pondering: "You can't get away from me—I've tried."

"I love it when you see somebody coming out of the bathroom laughing. Then they go back to the table and tell everyone.

"There are good drawings, too. There's one in the men's room right now that's going on the next shirt. It says: 'Is Magic Johnson related to Magic Marker?' It shows a magic marker in basketball shoes twirling a ball."

The men's room walls were being repainted a pale cream. "Someone took a Magic Marker to the men's room. He just ruined it. Usually we repaint every eight to ten months, just to get some new flavor. One result is better graffiti. Some of the best will be circled and left up. A fresh wall is pretty intimidating. You get more on a wall that already has slogans. That's why we leave a few things up. It spurs you on, if you have that brilliant midnight revelation."

But you'll never get credit for it. Bathroom graffiti is a lonely but democratic art form.

Blueberry Hill's "Take me drunk—I'm home again" has entertained people nightly, but the author will never be personally applauded.

"Most slogans come from somewhere else," Joe said, "but they had to make them up sometime. I like to think some of them started here."

84. The Secret Life of Aunt Emily

Every family used to have an Aunt Emily. She was a "career girl." That's what people called working women in those days. Emily was never married, except to her job. She was a bookkeeping whiz for a downtown business.

Emily dressed for her own kind of success. She wore sensible shoes and shapeless brown clothes. She had prim glasses and kept her hair in a short, practical frizz.

That's how a career woman was supposed to look. We heard that Aunt Emily was a genius with numbers. But she didn't age well. By the time I came along she was an eccentric figure who talked incessantly and walked with a slight stoop.

Any young woman in our family who wanted a career had to fight Aunt Emily's image. "It's OK to work until you get married," older relatives cautioned. "But you don't want to turn out like Aunt Emily."

After her retirement, Emily lived with her widowed sister in a house of terrifying cleanliness. The floors were so smooth and polished you expected someone to issue ice skates at the door. Each window had lace curtains and an ivory shade with its own crocheted pull. Lined up exactly under the pull was a small vase of yellowing wax flowers.

Aunt Emily had no dogs, cats or birds. I never heard music play in the house. The only sound was the solemn ticking of the old German clock in the kitchen.

Emily hated children. She considered them drooling, dripping masses who left fingerprints on her windows and dropped things on her floor. We children saw Aunt Emily twice a year, at Christmas and Easter. She waited for our invasion armed with a crumb brush. While we ate at the kitchen table, Aunt Emily stood by, brush in hand, and swept up anything that hit the floor.

The adults didn't like visiting Aunt Emily any more than we kids did. But at least they could face her with an anesthetic. Aunt Emily disapproved of drunkenness, but she did permit a holiday drink. She made only one, but that was all you needed. Lord knows how old Aunt Emily's bourbon was, but the stuff had started to crystalize. Long bourbon stalagmites formed on the bottom of her cut-glass decanter. One drink of Emily's semi-solid booze and she looked a lot better.

Once, when I was eight years old, Aunt Emily gave me a gift. It was a box of watercolors.

"Don't play around with them," she said warned. "Use them only to make great paintings."

That doomed the gift from the start. I made a few mud-colored splotches on the paper, decided I was no Michelangelo, and put the paint-box on a shelf.

We thought we knew all about Aunt Emily. She was an old maid who spent her days in a sterile round of newspaper reading, grocery shopping, church-going and house cleaning.

But Aunt Emily had a surprise for us when she died. We found a closet packed with beautiful, frivolous clothes: Colorful coats. Romantic hats with long feathers. Tiaras and necklaces fit for a fancy ball.

None of it had ever been worn. There, packed in mothballs and plastic, was the life she never lived.

85. Cheap Cuts

I can let you in on a fashion secret. There's a way to save money with style. I heard about it from Todd, a waiter in the stylish West End. He stays on the cutting edge of fashion. When ponytails were chic, Todd had one. Now he has a flattop.

But Todd used his head for this cut. He didn't go to an expensive stylist.

"A flattop would have cost me 50 bucks in the West End—$40 for the cut and $10 for the tip," he said. "God knows what they do to you if you don't tip. But I found a place on the South Side that did it for $3.50."

It was an old city barber shop, with "a striped pole out front, combs in that mysterious blue solution and old *Field & Stream* magazines. Just like the barber shop I went to when I was a little boy."

Why get a fashionable cut in such an unfashionable place?

"Very simple," said Todd, pouring more coffee. "This cut requires precision. Why go to a fashionable salon, where the stylist has done maybe two dozen of these cuts, when I can get a South Side barber who's done 10,000 flattops since the fifties? He's an artist. And he only charges $3.50.

"Besides, the South Side shop has such ambience. There was a man in the shop wearing a dirty T-shirt who claims to eat hair."

Todd's regulars, who listened raptly to this recital over breakfast, shuddered.

"I grew up on the East Coast," Todd said. "The South Side is so real."

To set the record straight, this isn't Todd's first flattop.

"They've been around a while. I've already had one, and had it grow out. But I got one this time because I'd just finished tying up some loose ends from my divorce. I needed to strip myself clean. It was either cut

off all my hair or run around naked.

"Everyone has had something to say about my cut," Todd said, delivering a toasted bagel. He leaned against a chair back, until a regular asked for more coffee.

"When you work in a restaurant, you're in the public eye," he said. "So many men had flattops years ago. They told me all about the time they got theirs. All the women say they want their husbands to get a cut like mine. But they don't really. If their husbands came home looking like this, they'd die.

"Most people like it. Only one person said straight out, 'I like you better with long hair.'

"Some said, 'Did you get your hair cut?' You could tell they didn't like it, but they weren't going to say so.

"Some asked if it was by choice. I tell those, 'I got busted and the police cut my hair.' Or, 'They wouldn't let me teach Sunday school unless I cut my hair.' Most people like the second reason better."

Todd said lots of stylish young men go to old city barbers for flattops. "They just won't admit it. It's the only way to go. Some of those old shops only charge $1.50 for a haircut. But I prefer the more expensive ones that give you a flattop for $3.50. After all, you get what you pay for."

You can say that with a straight face?

"Absolutely," Todd said. "I gave the barber a ten and told him to keep the change. I still saved $40. You can't get a flattop any cheaper than that."

"Yes, you can," said Louie, one of Todd's regulars. "Join the Marines."

86. *Halloween Humor Hits Bottom*

Every year, I wait for Halloween. That's when hundreds of little monsters come by my city house for candy.

This year, I took a certain evil pleasure in watching hordes of young Freddies from *Nightmare on Elm Street* swarm down my own street, trying to hold their loot in greedy, knife-blade fingers.

And all the little Jasons, who'd crawled out of the movie *Friday the 13th,* were wrestling with their white plastic masks and falling up my front steps. But besides all the entertainment Halloween costumes provide, kids also tell jokes. That's where St. Louis is different from many other cities. In some benighted places, the little children come to your home, yell, "Trick or treat" and people give them candy.

This system has no class. The kids might as well come to your door and say, "Stick 'em up." And in a few years, some of them will.

But St. Louisans never give anything away. This city was founded by the French and overrun by the Germans—and neither bunch is known

for generosity. So when you say "Trick or treat" here, it means just that. The kid has to tell a joke, a riddle, or do a tap dance. Only then will we fork over a piece of candy. Otherwise, tough luck, kid. Leftover Hershey bars can be frozen.

St. Louis kids tell great jokes. They know all three elements for quality humor: They are funny, dirty and tasteless. And the sweeter the kids look, the more likely they are to deliver a real shocker.

One of my favorite racy jokes was delivered by an angelic blond child.

"What's a French breakfast?" she asked, smiling shyly.

We didn't know.

"A roll in bed with honey."

That's why this Halloween was such a bust. The kids couldn't tell a joke—clean or dirty. One after another, they flubbed their lines.

Don H. and I dispensed candy from our front porch, and watched the depressing spectacle. Here's a sample:

"What are the colors of the ghost flag?" one kid asked.

Tell us, we said.

"Red, white and blue," the kid said.

"Huh?" said Don H. "I don't get it."

I did. As anyone who reads this column knows, I am an expert on bad jokes. The kid got the punch line wrong. He should have said the ghost flag was "Red, white and boo."

The next kid was a chipper little guy in a yellow monster suit. I had high hopes for him.

"Wanna hear a joke?" he volunteered.

Sure.

"A boy fell down in the mud."

His embarrassed parents pulled him off the porch like a vaudeville emcee with a hook.

Don H. was even more puzzled. "Did I miss something?" he said.

No, the kid did. He should have said, "Wanna hear a dirty joke?" Then it makes sense.

It went like that all night. More than a hundred kids mangled jokes on our porch. It was an endless open-mike night at a bad comedy club. There was one moment when it looked like things were about to improve. A child with dark, ringleted hair climbed up to the porch.

"Why did the whorehouse have so many long-distance phone calls?" she said, sweetly.

We don't know. But you're off to a good start.

"Because the ghosts made so many ghost-to-ghost phone calls."

"What are ghosts doing in a house like that?" whispered Don H., as she took her loot down the steps.

The kid had the wrong kind of house. It was supposed to be a haunted house.

The rest of the night was so awful, I almost wrote off Halloween '88. Had the younger generation lost the ability to deliver the shockeroo? I was all set to write an article on "What's Wrong with Today's Youth."

Then Gene Lewis called me the morning after Halloween. Gene restored my faith in the city's young people.

"I live in South St. Louis," Gene said. "I was handing out candy to the kids. The jokes this year were just awful. They seem to be getting worse.

"Anyway, three kids came up on my porch. One boy was about twelve. He wasn't wearing a costume, just some gray-looking sweats and bum's makeup. The first two told some awful jokes and I passed out their candy.

"Then the kid in the sweats said, 'Trick or treat.'

" 'What's your trick or riddle?' I asked.

"The kid said, 'What's the opposite of the sun?'

" 'I don't know.'

" 'The moon,' said the kid.

"He dropped his pants and mooned me right on my own front porch. Then he took off running into the night.

"It was the topper—or maybe that's the bottom—to my Halloween," he said.

I take my hat off to the kid, Gene. But that's all.

87. Buried in the Basement

Recently I went downstairs to the basement, opened a white metal cabinet and found seven cans of dried-up paint. The cabinet was next to the world's largest pair of rusty hedge clippers. The clippers were on top a pile of holey garden hoses. Tangled in the hoses were three plumber's helpers.

Every time the sink clogs up, I go out and buy a new plumber's helper. It doesn't help, so I take it downstairs, and lose it in the octopus tangle of hoses. Then I call the real plumber.

I never finished cleaning the basement that day. And I sure didn't find anything useful down there.

But Lee the Rehabber did. After thirty minutes in his basement, he came up with this system to classify people who stuff stuff in their basements.

"I dream of cleaning everything out," Lee said. "But actually doing it is a nightmare. I worked away for about half an hour cleaning the basement, before the twenty-year-old dust stirred up my asthma and I went out for a beer. But I got to thinking about basements. So I made a list."

Here are Lee's five types of basement savers:

Sally Spotless: "She doesn't collect anything, except family pictures and old birthday and Christmas cards," he said. "The pictures are in labeled albums, and the cards are boxed according to years. Her closets are always neat and she throws out the morning paper at noon.

"Her basement is cleaner than my living room. When she has to store something, like the Christmas ornaments and the artificial tree, she puts them in flowered storage boxes."

Sue the Saver: "Her house is tidy, but she has a huge box for coupons. She even saves coupons for things she doesn't use. Cat food, for instance. She doesn't have a cat, but someone she knows might get one.

"Sue has a monster collection of butter containers and microwave plastic plates. She never throws them away. After all, you never know when you might need one. Or a hundred.

"Sue's basement is neat, but loaded. Everything is boxed, bagged and labeled. She has Great-Aunt Kate's quilt and all the curtains from the first house she and her husband Sam bought thirty years ago. She still has her aluminum Christmas tree.

"Sam's workbench has every screw from everything he ever tried to fix. Sam has all the tools to do the job, but he never gets around to it."

Fred the Fixer: "He's not married, and the house is a mess," Lee said. "Fred washes his dishes once a week, vacuums once a month, and has every magazine he ever bought. His garage hasn't had room for the car since the week after he moved in."

Instead, it's stuffed with twelve lawn mowers (only two work), odd pipes and lumber, and broken appliances he's going to fix some day.

"His basement is a huge workshop. He can fix anything and he always has the parts. He has projects to keep him busy until he's 120."

Antique Anne: "She's an antique collector, so at least Anne has a reason for her madness. Her basement is full of old tools."

So is everyone else's.

"I mean pre-Civil War saws and axes," Lee said.

Anne's kitchen is a mess. She's never heard of a Cuisinart. "But she does have a mixer—with no cord. The toaster only toasts one side of bread at a time." There's nothing wrong with the toaster. It's another antique. That's how they used to make toast.

"Half of Anne's kitchen gadgets haven't been seen by people under thirty-five. The living room is packed with old rockers, uncomfortable carved chairs and a Victorian sofa. The lamps have wiring so old, you're scared to turn them on."

The bedroom must be a real trip.

"I haven't seen it," Lee said. "And I don't want to."

Equal time, now. Here's a peek into the basement of Lee the Rehabber:

"My basement is filled with boxed dishes, old clothes, and more paint cans than Central Hardware. I have fifteen old doors. I don't know what to do with them, but they're too good to throw away. I've got storm windows that don't belong on my house. But they're too good to throw away, too.

"Oh, I forgot the garden hose. It has the end that you hook up to the faucet torn off."

Any plumber's helpers?

"No, they don't work," Lee said. "I use a can of Drano. Then when that fails I call the plumber."

88. A Dirty Little Story

This is a dirty little story, but Martha Ferguson likes to tell it. "St. Louis people brag about how clean they keep their houses," she said. "They say you can eat off their kitchen floors."

Not me. We have a table.

"Whenever someone talks about how clean her house is, I think of Gladys May," Martha said. "When I was growing up, Gladys kept the cleanest house in the neighborhood."

What did she look like?

"I'm not sure. I never saw her face. Gladys cleaned her floors so much, she was always stooped over. Either she was scrubbing them. Or putting down fresh newspapers to protect the floors. Or taking up the newspapers, so she could scrub the floors again.

"Come to think of it, I never saw Gladys' floors, either. She mopped and waxed her kitchen floor daily. The newspapers kept them clean. I think she sterilized the papers in an autoclave.

"The bathroom was equally spotless. Gladys even had a little sign over the toilet-paper holder, saying how many sheets you could use."

In those days, during the depression, women competed with each other to see how clean they could keep their houses. Parties of housewives met for coffee in one another's homes, and quietly inspected for dust in the corners and on top the furniture.

Gladys did many things the standard house-proud woman did: She attacked the dirt in the corners with a knife. She ran a knife along the break in the leaves of the kitchen table to remove crumbs. She took down her curtains in the house and starched them every week.

But Gladys always did one better than the rest of the neighborhood.

"She took down the garage curtains and washed them weekly, too. She thought the garage's concrete floors looked dirty, so she put down linoleum. She mopped and waxed the garage linoleum every week, and then covered it with fresh newspapers."

Gladys saw her husband off to work every day, as any good wife did then. She followed him out to the garage. But it wasn't just from affection.

"When her husband took his car out of the garage to drive to work, Gladys went out and changed the garage newspapers."

The neighbors were amazed. But they were more amazed one day when "we found Gladys May wandering in her nightgown, six miles from home. She'd gone clean out of her mind.

"That was many years ago. Gladys is gone now, I suppose, to scrub up in heaven," Martha said. "Unless they've put her to work cleaning up the other place."

89. Say It Again, Sam

South Side Rich said, "Our language doesn't seem as colorful any more."

You should have been in the bar I was Saturday night. When the air turned blue, it wasn't from the cigarette smoke.

"I don't mean dirty," Rich said. "I mean interesting. Now you hear business talk, like 'bottom line.' And computer terms, like 'down time' and 'debug.' Debug is a six-legged insect you find in de plants.

"People used to use such great phrases. I remember my grandparents using them. You don't hear them any more. They're dying out. You never said anybody was dumb. You'd say, 'You're so dumb your brain rattles like a BB in a boxcar.'"

I heard the BB was in a rain barrel.

"Whatever," Rich said. "It had great alliteration.

"When your grandfather was broke, he didn't say he was experiencing a shortfall. He said, 'If a nickel could take you around the world, I couldn't get out of town.'"

Some old phrases were as ornate and flowery as a Victorian parlor. Others were sharp, short and funny—automatic responses to common problems. Rich rattled them off:

"What do you have for dinner after a family fight?" he asked.

Cold shoulder and hot tongue.

"What do you call a Saturday spent working around the house?" That's a Honey-Do Day: "Honey, do this. Honey, do that."

"And what if you questioned something your mother did?" Rich said. "Suppose she smoked cigarettes, but wouldn't let you light up. If you said anything, she'd answer: 'Don't do as I do, do as I say.' Maybe it wasn't great child psychology, but it was a lot better than a wimpy, 'Because I'm the Mom.'"

Something really disgusting would "gag a maggot on a gut wagon."

"Something really spiffy (no one says that any more, either) was 'just like downtown.' I used to like my mashed potatoes perfect, with a little bowl in the center to hold the gravy. When I arranged them that way, it was 'just like downtown.' ''

That must have been before urban blight.

'' 'Just like the mall' is not the same,'' Rich said.

When your aunts described someone who was overdressed, they'd say: ''She flounced in, dressed up like Astor's plush horse.''

''People flounced a lot more in those days,'' Rich said. ''They didn't just walk into a room.

''Astor is one of those vanished names. There are more. When someone was throwing money around, you'd say: 'Who do you think you are—Rockefeller?'

''Anyone who went fast drove like Barney Oldfield.

''And hunks had muscles like Charles Atlas.''

Those were the good old days. Atlas is a lot easier to spell than Schwarzenegger.

''A fat woman was as big as the *Queen Mary*. Nobody says anyone is as big as the *Queen Elizabeth II*.

''Some old phrases don't make sense any more,'' Rich said. ''If a person was really poor, my mother would say they didn't have 'enough money to buy an ant a wrestling jacket.' I never knew what a wrestling jacket was, or why you put it on an ant.''

I never figured out why someone was independent as a pig on ice. Or had more brass than a government mule.

Why would a woman set her cap for a man, when her head was the last thing she would use to catch him?

Some of those phrases had to be cleaned up for company. My favorite was: ''He's so dumb he couldn't pour water out of a boot with the directions written on the heel.''

''That's sort of how I heard it,'' Rich said. ''I'll clean up another one: If baloney was a brass band, you'd play all the time.''

If someone was a fast talker he could talk the balls off . . .

''Careful,'' Rich said.

A pool table.

90. Born to Lose

''I always thought you had to take risks to succeed,'' D. J. Fone said. ''It turns out you have to take them to fail, too.''

D. J. didn't really fail. But a lot of the companies he worked for did. He swears this story is true.

D. J. says he worked his way through junior college loading trucks. ''Two truck lines went out of business,'' he said. ''That should have been a clue. So I took a summer job with an auto parts broker. That, too, went under before the summer was over. But, hey, this stuff happens.

"I finished my degree and got a promising job at the Shoppers Fair discount store in far North County. It closed two months later.

"But my boss liked my work and took me along to the Shoppers Fair store in Normandy. Six months later that, too, was history. But retail is risky, right?"

D. J. tried the restaurant business. "Burger Chef hired me as an assistant manager, then placed me at the lowest-grossing store in the chain. About a year later, a former store manager filed a minor complaint against me, and D. J. Fone was history. But a year later, so was Burger Chef. Now it's called Hardee's.

"So I thought about more lucrative career options. Like my own record store. First, I got a job at Peaches to learn the business. Shortly after that, Peaches was picked up by Sound Warehouse.

"But a guy's gotta work. I headed to where the jobs were—a downtown hotel. This looked like a real career opportunity. It was. I had two promotions in a year.

"What paved the way for the quick promotions was the mass leaving of executives who learned the hotel's food operations were being merged by the new owner."

Once again, D. J. was out of a job. "But food service is pretty high risk. I decided to pursue the career I really wanted: Sportscasting."

He took a job at an Italian restaurant, and worked his way through broadcast school. Soon D. J. had a real job offer, sportscasting at an Oklahoma radio station.

"I moved 700 miles in four days. There was just one problem. When I got there, the sportscasting job suddenly became filled. All that was open was a sales job. No local wanted it. With good reason. Less than a year later, the town's biggest employer closed."

D. J. took another radio job in dusty southwest Kansas. After three months, the station was suddenly out of business, "taken over by a rival in a bitter court battle."

But D. J. Fone thought his luck was about to change. "Just before leaving for Kansas, I got a call from a former KMOX sports announcer. He raved over my hockey tapes. He said he'd turn them over to his influential buddy, Jack Carney." The biggest name in St. Louis radio.

"I returned from Kansas just in time to hear about Carney's untimely death. Even I didn't think my luck was that bad."

There's more, but it's almost too painful to repeat. In the winter of 1985, D. J.'s old Kansas radio boss offered him a job in Oklahoma. And a job for D. J.'s wife. "Turns out the station was deep in debt. So was the town. Six months later, the station was history. So was my marriage."

D. J. went back to the Italian restaurant. Then he got a great offer at an Ozark station. He was deliriously happy. For four months. Then this station also bit the dust. So did the job he took with a local employer.

"Once again, back to St. Louis. Once again, back to the restaurant business. This time to an eatery that was . . . sold to a new partner within a few months.

"So I decided to take some time off. Live off my savings. I took my bank book down to the trusty, solid place where I'd banked for years— Bohemian Savings."

The feds closed it in 1987.

Can I ask a favor, D. J.? If you ever get a job where I work, could you give me sixty days' notice?

91. MOM Goes to the Movies

South Side Rich is worried. "Today's movies are ruining kids' minds," he said. "They give kids an unrealistic view of life."

Do you think the sex and violence will warp their lives?

"I'm not worried about their lives. It's mine. Thanks to the movies, my kid thinks my life is more exciting than it really is.

"It was bad enough when *Flashdance* came out. Remember that one? The gorgeous young woman who was a welder by day and a dancer at night? My kid thought I should hang around discos and find a nice lady welder. I tried to explain that most welders, male and female, are too tired to go dancing after a hard day at work. And many of them have tattoos.

"Then *Dirty Dancing* came out. My kid said, 'Did you dance like that in 1963?'

"I told him 1963 was still the fifties and nobody did anything. The teachers would have crucified us on the school lawn if we even thought of dancing like that. We had chaperones at our dances. We couldn't even dance close together. The chaperones would watch you during slow dances to make sure there was room enough to put a hand between you."

The chaperone's hand. Not the dancer's.

"Besides, girls were buttoned up in those days. They couldn't wear low-cut dresses. And they all had girdles, even if they didn't need them. They couldn't bend the way people did in that movie."

Rich's son was not impressed by this history lesson. "The kid didn't believe me, but at least he quit asking questions.

"Then I saw the previews for the Tom Cruise movie, *Cocktail*. That's the one where the bartender is so good he flips bottles up in the air while he makes drinks. While he's throwing the liquor, beautiful women are throwing themselves at him. I know some women act that way around bartenders, but the ones I saw don't look like movie stars. Their fathers didn't have millions of dollars, either.

"Anyway, I went for a drink after the show. It's a place near the movie theater, and the bartender's flipping the bottles up in the air, just like Tom Cruise.

"I was terrified. It was like being in a bar during the Blitz. I had to duck while I drank. I've had drinks that would knock you to the floor, but usually they're on the outside of the bottle. Think of the breakage going on in bars all over the country. Can America afford any more movies like this?"

Probably not. That's why I think it's time for my Monitor Our Movies (MOM) Committee. MOM would not interfere with the film script or production in any way. MOM would simply review the movie. If the committee decided it was wildly wrong, MOM would require that a warning be flashed on the screen before the movie was shown.

Dirty Dancing would carry one something like this: "WARNING: The dirty dancing in this film never actually happened to anyone living in 1963. But the writer and director wish it had."

MOM would be allowed to correct historically inaccurate films if persons from that period were still alive and would be embarrassed by the movie. Many fifties nostalgia films could carry this: "WARNING: No nice girl dated a man who looked like Elvis Presley in the 1950s. Not with her parents' permission, anyway."

The MOM Committee could also point out when professions were inaccurately portrayed. MOM could use a blanket warning, like this one: "WARNING: Doctors, (teachers, lawyers, nurses, police officers) are not as bad or good as the ones in this movie. Mediocrity is the rule in any profession."

MOM would not only condemn. MOM could also approve certain films. Especially if they were extremely truthful.

"I was in the army," Rich said. "The movie *Dr. Strangelove* was not funny. It was real."

92. *The City Guide to Beer Etiquette*

Once again, I am asked to answer a city etiquette question. The situation arose at a fashionable downtown party, where the guests were served beer and White Castles.

The city's bar society scarfed up the suds and sliders. But some underprivileged party goers, who usually eat things like warm duck salad and vegetable pate, were unfamiliar with the menu.

They figured out the White Castles in a hurry. Soon elegantly dressed people were carrying tiny plates balanced with Belly Bombers, stuffed mushroom caps and other dainty hors d'oeuvres.

But a debate broke out among the quiche and kiwi crowd about the beer. They wanted to know, "How do you drink a long neck?"

The party's so-called experts delivered really bum advice. They said since a beer bottle is called a "long neck," you should hold it by the neck.

This breach of etiquette horrified the bar society at the party. They kept quiet, knowing that polite people do not correct guests, even if they are holding bottles of Busch by the neck, with one pinkie extended.

But the issue continued to brew. The next day, I received a call. I will now endeavor to answer this important city etiquette question: "How do you drink a long neck?"

First, never call a beer a long neck. In Northern cities, only Texans and other undesirables, such as yuppies who drink beer with lime, call a bottle of beer a long neck.

The proper way to request a bottle of brew in a saloon is: "Gimme a beer."

A good bartender knows a beer comes in a bottle with a long neck. Otherwise, the customer would have said, "Gimme a draft."

No self-respecting bartender ever serves canned beer.

Now that you know what to call it, you need to know how to hold it.

The answer is simple. By the body. This is not high school dating— it's OK to go below the neck. In fact, it is right and proper. That is why beer bottles have labels, so you can grasp them and keep your hands reasonably dry.

When the label sweats through and your palm gets wet, it's time to change into another dry beer.

Never, never hold a beer by the neck in a bar. This is a threatening gesture. It means you're spoiling for a fight, and will shortly knock the neck off the bottle and begin the festivities.

At this point, trained bartenders bring out their own "long necks"— wooden sticks or pipes filled with lead—and begin thumping you about the head and shoulders while phoning for the police.

There is only one time when you can hold a beer by the neck. That's when you're outside, at a picnic. This type of necking indicates an informal atmosphere.

If you decide to do further in-depth beer drinking research, remember: No true beer lover ever orders a light beer, unless you have a headache and the bartender is out of Alka-Seltzer.

Light beer commercials are great, but real beer drinkers don't want to diet. They are proud of their beer guts. These are symbols of adulthood. A good beer gut takes years to perfect. It is not fat and sloppy. It is round and tight as a kettle drum, which it resembles in size, shape and sound.

Along with the beer, you will encounter many interesting bar foods: boneless chicken (pickled eggs in a glass jar), beef jerky, and small pizzas which taste remarkably like the box they came in. These foods are ordered only after several beers.

Also, after a few beers you can begin doing beer tricks. One of the most impressive is bending beer caps with your bare fingers. There's a knack to this, and when I've had a few beers I'll show you.

I know a man who married a woman who could bend beer caps with her fingers. He was deeply impressed by her display of strength in the local saloon.

Actually, he was afraid not to marry her.

I think it was because she removed the caps with her teeth.

93. The New South

My South Side neighborhood is changing. Each day, a little of it seems to disappear: A small stand of white-trimmed red brick houses is cut down. Overnight, a new Taco Bell, McDonald's, or muffler shop springs up in their place.

In the morning, the old women still come out to do their shopping, armed with wire grocery carriers and sturdy black purses. Older South Side women come in two sizes: Tall, thin, iron-haired ones, with straight backs and black Enna Jettick shoes. And short, dumpy grandmotherly women, with figures like fat flour sacks tied in the middle. You can tell they will have comforting, flabby arms and wide, generous laps.

The old men still go out for their evening walks. You see them in their neatly pressed baggy pants, pulled up high. They have long hairy ears and big cigars. They do not have the pink and silver look of rich old men, yet they are powerful in their own way.

As you watch their dignified progress down the streets, you know that soon they too will vanish.

And who will take their place?

Their sons and daughters have long since fled to the suburbs and grown old. They will not come back. They hated the South Side. To them, it is old, nosy, and confined. They escaped the city, and they're proud of it.

Now a few of their children, the old people's grandchildren, are coming back to the city. They are a perverse breed, who found their parents' orderly suburban paradise a cold and colorless hell.

Our grandparents' city, with its old brick houses and dark old saloons smelling of Lysol and stale beer, is exotic.

The rainy nights are romantic. The streets are dark and unnaturally quiet. The cars go by with a shushing sound. The street lights shimmer and light up the glossy wet leaves. The city alleys have rain-slicked bricks and drooping, water-drenched roses.

At night, the air has a rich, warm, sour smell from the brewery.

In the early morning, on your way to work, you'll see the gaudy streaks of sunrise light up the gray roofs, and smell the warm, buttery bread from the bakery.

We are glad to be home, but we know we are not like those old South Siders. It is their doing. They made us different.

Many of them never finished high school, some never got through grade school.

They went to work in City Hall, in the city businesses, as clerks and secretaries and middle managers. Others went to work in factories and gas stations, ran the saloons and the shops.

They were good employees. They worked hard. They were loyal. They were conscientious.

They were often laughed at by the very people who took advantage of these virtues. You could count on the South Siders to stay late, to keep things clean, to work themselves even to an early grave—and to get only so far.

They had inside a bitterness and an anger and a wicked sense of humor.

These were their weapons in their harsh world—but they were also their undoing when they tried to get free of it. They did not have the easy social skills that could start them on the long upward climb.

But they believed in education. That was their real religion. School was salvation. Even the old people who never got past the fourth grade wanted culture. They subscribed to the *National Geographic* and the *Reader's Digest*. And they encouraged us to improve ourselves.

So we did. We are, most of us, the first generation to graduate from college. This is a source of pride to our families, and a source of distance, too.

We became the people they didn't quite trust: the lawyers, the doctors, the writers, the bosses who used them.

We talked different.

We liked strange foods. Instead of good, well-cooked roasts and boiled vegetables, we developed a taste for Thai food, spicy Indian cooking, Chinese stir fries. We did not buy the cheaper cuts of meat. We never ate sausage and cabbage or sauerkraut and neckbones—"puzzle bones" the old people called them. We did not use up all our leftovers.

We did not have their gift for saving. The old people took one vacation a year—a week at a lodge in the Missouri Ozarks. They did not run down to Cancun or go to China. They did not take weekend trips to Chicago.

They did not buy a car until they could pay cash for it. They often paid cash for their houses, too.

They could afford to. They never squandered money on babysitters and dinners out. They stayed in and saved.

And, we secretly thought, threw away their youth.

And when they died, those stodgy old people in the baggy pants and polyester pantsuits left surprisingly large estates—sometimes half a million dollars or more, the fruits of eating in, shopping for the cheapest orange juice, buying clothes only on sale.

The money went to their children in the suburbs.

Their neighborhood will go to their grandchildren—their real grandchildren, or their spiritual ones.

We bought our red brick house from a woman who refused to sell it to her brother. She suspected he'd turn around and sell it again for a fat profit.

"You kids can have it," she said. "You love it."

That scene was repeated all around the neighborhood: The old would size up the young couples and give their houses to the ones who would take care of them.

The old were surprisingly canny. They had no qualms about selling to gays, yuppies, Asian refugees—all people South Siders might normally despise—if they thought you were sufficiently house proud.

Then they laid a terrible burden on us. "You can have my house," they said. "You'll take care of it."

Suddenly, we weren't buying, we were adopting.

And we began to adopt their values, even as we laughed at them. We didn't scrub the porch steps with Old Dutch cleanser—but we kept them preternaturally clean. We laughed at the old ladies who got up at 6 A.M. to pick the fallen leaves off their zoysia. But we trimmed our grass.

We started painting a lot more often, and found ourselves frowning at the neighborhood slobs when they parked their rustbuckets in front of our houses.

We were turning into some strange mutation: the new South Sider. We wouldn't be caught dead with an aluminum awning. But we had canvas ones.

We bought pink flamingos and twirling plastic sunflowers as jokes—but we put them on our lawns, and unless you really saw us, you didn't know if we belonged to the old or the new South.

We called ourselves liberals. But sometimes we called the city inspector on anyone we thought wasn't keeping their place up. After all, we had to protect our property values.

The new South Siders put in Jacuzzis and sun decks and storm windows.

Our street is changing. You'll see some strange sights now in my old, once insular neighborhood—Vietnamese women wearing black pajamas and carrying paper umbrellas. But they carry their shopping bags, like proper South Side women.

Yet when it rains, my neighborhood still looks like it did fifty years ago.

The heavy, water-drenched roses still hang over the alley fences. The air has the rich, sour brewery smell.

The old people still go for their slow stately walks.

And we are right behind them.

ELAINE VIETS, author of *Urban Affairs,* has been writing a column for the *St. Louis Post-Dispatch* since 1978. She was nominated for a Pulitzer Prize for co-authoring a five-part series on the Church of Scientology. As the host and writer of a nationally syndicated radio show, the "Travel-Holiday Magazine," she is heard in 200 cities coast to coast. She is married to Don Crinklaw and lives in South St. Louis. This is her third book.